Virginia Cyr

God's Little Hobo

Virginia Cyr

God's Little Hobo

By Virginia Cyr

**Edited by
Quentin Colgan, Ph.D.**

Our Sunday Visitor Publishing Division
Our Sunday Visitor, Inc.
Huntington, Indiana 46750

Our Sunday Visitor Publishing Division
Our Sunday Visitor, Inc.
200 Noll Plaza
Huntington, IN 46750

ISBN: 1-59276-024-4 (Inventory No. T75)
LCCN: 2003113168

Cover design by Rebecca J. Heaston
Photos courtesy of Quentin Colgan, with special thanks to Julie Barrett, Marg McGuire and Velma Osting.
Interior design by Sherri L. Hoffman

PRINTED IN THE UNITED STATES OF AMERICA

*To my wife, Ellie,
in admiration, for all she has endured and achieved.*

Contents

Introduction

ion

ABOUT HER LIFE

---

*I*t is late at night at Good Samaritan Nursing Home in Kokomo, Indiana. The date is October 23, 1963. An aide makes the rounds of the patients' rooms. All is still except for an occasional moan or cough. At one end of the hallway a glow radiates from a small corner room, and the click of a typewriter stroke can be heard as a young woman gains enough control of her palsied hand to direct it to the desired keys. Patiently, laboriously, she types another letter to the Blessed Mother. More often than not, she is incredibly exhausted, usually too tired for sleep; almost always she is wracked with pain. But pain and fatigue are no match for a love that must be expressed. Slowly she types out: "Mother, here at last I may be with you. It is such a joy. I just know you love my little corner, the pretty music in the background, the peck of Anita [*her typewriter*], all the friendly little treasures that surround me here. I love typing letters to you, seeing your sweet smile, cuddling close to your heart, being with you in the silence that is God. Thank you for being always here to embrace all that is heaven, and earth, in me."

Virginia's life was marked by cerebral palsy, institutional living and, to some extent, loneliness. Yet these served merely as a crucible that purified her life and her longings. And from that crucible was born a rare and beautiful creature, one filled with wit and wisdom, passion and insight; a woman blessed

9

superabundantly by God with the Christian virtues of faith, hope, and love.

Virginia Cyr was born on May 10, 1942, in Indianapolis, Indiana. She reports in her journals that she was baptized the same day; perhaps an indication of a premature or traumatic birth. At the age of four, Virginia began to manifest signs of cerebral palsy. It was at this time that her mother abandoned the family, leaving Virginia and her younger brother, Jimmy, under the care of her father, Oliver (Red) Cyr.

Of her earliest years, Virginia writes: "When I was a baby, not even a day old, my loving Father in heaven tapped me on the shoulder and asked me if I'd like to do something special for Him. I was just bursting with enthusiasm, and in my timid, baby way, I accepted the challenge. And what a challenge it was, and is, bringing disappointments, but far outnumbered by physical and spiritual joys.

Virginia at seventeen months, with her father

"As can be expected of babies, I soon started growing, doing some of the feats and antics expected of babies, not accomplishing others. Then came the comparing. Mother talked with other mothers; Daddy called home every once in a while to see what I had accomplished. I'm afraid I really disappointed them. Of course, they didn't know my secret, that special agreement between God and me."

Her childhood years were anything but happy. Again, she writes: "Deprived of our mother, Jimmy and I were placed in one foster home after another, a few nightmares for two frightened little ones.

"Next, Jimmy and I were taken to St. Vincent Villa orphanage in Fort Wayne [*Indiana*]. Wonderful joy and peace of childhood. Fantasies easily came true. And in this atmosphere, Jesus came to my heart for the first time [*in First Holy Communion*]. . . . From just fantasies back into the world of heartaches. One school after another, from house to house, never to a home."

Virginia spent her last two years of grade school at St. John's Crippled Children's School and Hospital in Springfield, Illinois. She graduated from the eighth grade in 1956, and was accepted into St. Joseph's Academy in Tipton, Indiana, for high school. During her senior year of high school, while deathly ill, Virginia had an experience that helped shape the rest of her life. She writes: "Overwork had brought me a very grave illness. Months in hospitals, all fifty-eight pounds of me struggling for a drop of strength, even my brain dehydrated so that I couldn't read or converse much. One day I lay there and saw a crucifix, and told Jesus if He wished He could leave me thus, always. But that was the day He chose to begin my return to health. He had awaited my abandonment, that's all."

Virginia graduated from St. Joseph Academy in 1960, and then spent two more years living and working there. She began her journals in February 1962, and continued them until November 1966, when she became too weak to write or dictate. From SJA, Virginia moved into Good Samaritan Hospital, a nursing home in Kokomo, Indiana. That was to be her earthly domicile until very near the end of her short life.

At the time I met Virginia, I was a junior monk, or *frater*, at St. Meinrad Archabbey in southern Indiana. During Holy Week in 1965, I was appointed to oversee the guesthouse because the senior monks were on retreat that week. On Wednesday of that week, Virginia's father brought Virginia to the guesthouse, got her settled in a room, and then left. I knew that the monks closest to Virginia were not free at that time, so I decided it was my "duty" to go over to her room and check in on the poor, unfortunate creature until her friends could free me of the obligation. That details roughly the state of my thinking as I made up my mind to pay her a visit. There was a sign I had to hang on the guesthouse office door, a sign with a clock face and movable hands: "Back at such and such a time." I certainly didn't intend to stay more than five minutes, so that is what I indicated on the sign.

I went down to Virginia's room, knocked on the door, and my life changed forever. I don't know exactly what I was expecting; perhaps some poor, unfortunate, lonely person who was handicapped to boot. What I encountered was an intelligent, lively, funny, attractive young lady. Probably one of the first things I noticed upon opening the door was that Virginia was seated on the floor, leaning against one of the beds. She was unable to sit up straight without support whenever she was not in her wheelchair. I made an almost instantaneous decision not to stand or sit on a level above her. I sat down on the floor opposite her, and we began to converse.

I don't remember after all these years what topics we may have touched upon in that first conversation; Virginia remembers that I offered her a drink of water. Ten minutes became twenty before I realized that I had indicated on the office door that I would be back at the office long since. I returned to the office, waited around long enough to convince myself that no one was in need of my services, changed the time on the sign, and returned to Virginia's room. I remember that I followed that procedure the remainder of the afternoon.

By the time I met Virginia, she had long since realized that her vocation was not to the religious life. She was, however, living a consecrated life, having taken vows privately. She came to the conviction that her calling was to *be with*, or perhaps more accurately, to *be for*, whoever invited her into their homes or lives. Thus she was always on the go, ready in an instant to pack up and spend time with anyone who sought her company. It was for this reason that she was lovingly referred to as, and often called herself, "God's little hobo."

When not traveling, her time was taken up with corresponding with those whom she met during her travels. Once people met Virginia, they felt an overwhelming desire to keep in touch with her. She considered this correspondence to be a vital part of her ministry. At the time of her death, her list of correspondents numbered three hundred twenty-five.

She was greatly attracted to the religious community known as the Little Brothers and Little Sisters of the Incarnation. This was a religious community founded in France, inspired by the example of Charles de Foucauld. Members of this community live among the poorest of the poor, in slums, in prisons, among pagans, Muslims, Hindus, Christians. Their apostolate is to give witness to the Gospel not by preaching and teaching, but by prayer, service, manual labor, and example. The symbol of their community is a heart, at the top of which is a cross. For the last several years of her life, every outfit that Virginia owned had that symbol sewn into it.

Among the facts that I learned about Virginia during that first visit was that she kept a journal, but it was no ordinary journal. Her entries were all addressed to Mary, the Mother of Jesus. She referred to them as her "Letters to Mother." Mary was a very important person in Virginia's life. Mary became, to some extent, the mother that Virginia never had. Anyone who reads her journals cannot help but be impressed by the tremendous love Virginia had for the Blessed Mother. I had known Virginia all of ten days when she entrusted to me all of the volumes of her journal, telling me that she *knew* I was the person who was supposed to have them.

By October 1966, Virginia's health was steadily declining. She was, in fact, dying. The Ted Kiefer family of Elwood, Indiana, took her into their home at this time. It was early December when Ruth Kiefer wrote me to ask if there was any way at all that I might get permission to leave the monastery for a day or two to visit Virginia. Virginia was dying, and she wished to see me one last time. Mrs. Kiefer's request was honored by my superiors, and I was allowed to visit Virginia. I was able to spend about twenty-four hours with her.

One room on the main floor of the Kiefers' home had been turned into Virginia's room. She was situated in a hospital bed that could be manipulated to contour the mattress. At the foot of Virginia's bed was an altar. I recall that I contributed a rough-hewn cross for the altar. I arrived about mid-afternoon at the Kiefers', and visited with Virginia and the family until late into the night. Virginia at this time was quite weak, but still very alert, still very lovely. The next morning, a Sunday, a priest friend of the family offered Mass in Virginia's room. Shortly after that, my ride came, and I had to say my good-byes.

I received word on February 3, 1967, that Virginia Cyr, Little Virginia of Jesus, God's little hobo, had finally arrived Home. It never occurred to me to pray for the repose of her soul. Upon hearing of her death, I began praying to her, for I knew that the dearest friend I had yet had in my life was now a saint in heaven.

About Her Spirituality

This is certainly not the place for an in-depth analysis of Virginia's spirituality, but a few pointers could be of considerable assistance to the reader. I would like to mention and comment upon two elements of her spirituality that I take to be central.

First of all, Virginia was greatly influenced by the life, example, and teaching of Charles de Foucauld. Although she was never officially accepted into the Secular Fraternity of the Little Sisters, she was an ardent advocate of his spirituality. Much of the imagery of her spirituality can be traced back to the writings of Brother Charles. Important among those images are the notion of desert, seeds to be planted for later flowering,

Nazareth, and the heart (love) surmounted by the cross (suffering).

I will take but one of those themes, the concept of Nazareth, as an illustration. For Brother Charles, the concept "Nazareth" stands for an ideal: the genuine realization of God's kingdom on earth, an intimate setting in which the Gospel message of love is fully embodied and lived. It was his conviction that there could be no better primer of spirituality for Christians than the hidden life of Jesus in Nazareth.

Brother Charles' concept of Nazareth was one that Virginia drew upon frequently. It became for her not only the term that identified a Christian ideal, but it was also the term she used for the only experience of family life she had ever had. Her summer with the Tanzillis *was* a summer in Nazareth. As a member of that loving family, she experienced the ideal in a very concrete setting. It is difficult for anyone who numbers the experience of family life in terms of decades to comprehend what that summer with the Tanzillis meant to Virginia, who numbered the experience of family life precisely in terms of those few weeks. It helps us to better understand Virginia's struggle when she left that Nazareth. Her vocation as God's little hobo was calling her away from that idyllic experience back to the harsh realities of institutional living. In Virginia's later writings, one can perhaps hear in the term "Nazareth" an echo of her longing for heaven, for Home.

The second element of her spirituality that I wish to consider requires a word or two of explanation. It is difficult to imagine anyone who was less encumbered by her handicap than Virginia, or anyone whose handicap restricted her activity less than Virginia's. Yet, her handicap did create limitations and tensions of one sort or another in her life. The one tension I wish to comment upon is best expressed biblically in the different vocations of Martha and Mary. Virginia desired with all her being *to be of service* to others, and to be of service in as active a way as she possibly could. She expresses herself ardently concerning this in a passage from February 14, 1963: "I thank God for every opportunity to go out among souls and bring His Presence there. I give of myself, my strength, my time, my Love, all the glorious experiences with which God has conditioned me for such a vocation. And I beg that this self I wish to be consumed in the multitudes may be none other than Christ. How else might I serve? I can't imagine another way for me, for there is no other way. Jesus asks that His life be thus in me. O the eternal tragedy of refusing! No, I can't refuse."

Yet the obstacles to such service, imposed by her cerebral palsy, were severe. Undoubtedly, she recognized the wisdom of a priest acquaintance's remarks to her concerning this. She writes: "When Father LeClerc was here, he told me that since my apostolate must be a limited one, I must back this great movement to the spirit of Brother Charles with my prayers. He has chosen me, and my role is that of sitting at His feet. I must never waste time by wishing for Martha's part. Mine is to sit there, and listen, and LOVE" (August 22, 1962).

It was because of this sense of not being able to do everything she wished to do in terms of an active ministry that her participation as a co-missionary in the work of her spiritual director and friend, Father Keith Hosey, was so important to her. She continues:

"[*Father LeClerc*] told me that he would give me a very special assignment for Brother Charles. He told me that I would back Father Keith in his tremendous apostolate. What a privilege! And I, who had prayed for him so much before, now tried to double these meager but sincere offerings for

Father Keith Hosey

him, knowing that God our Father would accept their lowliness because you, my Mother, would embellish them with your riches before you took such things of poverty to the divine majesty of the King" (August 22, 1962).

This second important element of Virginia's spirituality is revealed in the theology behind the idea of being a co-missionary. There is a belief in the Catholic Christian community that all the faithful are members of the Mystical Body of Christ. This belief from earliest times has been expressed in the words of the Apostles' Creed: "I believe in . . . the communion of saints." In *Mirae Caritatis* (On the Holy Eucharist), Pope Leo XIII writes: "As everyone knows, the communion of saints is nothing else than a mutual sharing in help, satisfaction, prayer, and other good works, a mutual communication among all the faithful. . . ." Hence, for example, the weakness manifest in one portion of the believing community can be fortified through the prayer, suffering, and sacrifices of another portion of that community.

Virginia Cyr, God's Little Hobo,
May 10, 1942-February 3, 1967

Virginia believed passionately in this teaching. At one point in her writings, she referred to it as "that vast doctrine which so often explains my joy and my anguish" (December 1, 1964). Thus, as Father Keith's co-missionary, Virginia offered her physical sufferings, her disappointments — even her weakness — so that Father Keith might be more effective in his ministry. It was a way for Virginia to participate more fully in the active ministry of the Church. As such, it was a very important part of her spirituality.

Other important elements of Virginia's spirituality — her devotion to the sacraments, her enthusiastic participation in the events and feasts of the Church year, her profound love of Mary, and her sensitivity to the presence of Christ in all people — will be readily evident to the reader.

And finally, by way of a personal note to you, the reader, I can attest to the fact that there are still alive today many who simply cannot forget the impact that one young woman, radiant with the love of God, had upon their lives oh so many years ago. That love, a love that touched so many, permeates the pages of Virginia's journal as well. And now you, too, perhaps out of curiosity, perhaps through word-of-mouth, may have picked up this book in much the same way I knocked on the guest-room door that day many years ago: completely oblivious of the moment of grace I was about to receive. My prayer is that you also find your life touched — perhaps even changed — by your encounter with Virginia Cyr, "God's little hobo."

QUENTIN COLGAN, PH.D.
Ohio Dominican University
Feast of All Saints
November 1, 2003

Editor's Note

⮜❧⮞

*V*irginia's journals, her "Letters to Mother," are contained in a set of nine loose-leaf notebooks. The notebooks contain eight-by-five typed, single-spaced pages, and are of varying length. There are nine hundred sixty-five such pages. When transcribed, those pages total close to twelve hundred double-spaced, printed pages. This volume presents about two hundred thirty of the original twelve hundred pages; a chapter is devoted to each of the nine notebooks, with the corresponding time frame given at the beginning of each chapter. Obviously, many significant incidents and relationships from her life had to be passed over, given the limited scope of this volume. While providing what I hope to be sufficient information about the externals of her life, I have chosen instead to highlight Virginia's spiritual journey — how she used the events and circumstances of her life as an ongoing invitation and opportunity to give herself ever more completely to God. In editing this work, I have attempted to retain the originality and flavor of Virginia's journal entries, and thus I have followed her syntax and spelling as much as possible.

When I have completed my work with these journals, I will donate them — as well as all other letters and papers in my possession that pertain to Virginia's life — to the St. Meinrad Archabbey Library, St. Meinrad, Indiana, where they will be available to others for continued research. It seems only fitting that her writings should eventually be returned to her beloved "Hobo Haven," the place where Virginia found so much peace, and from which she drew so much strength.

It is with thanks to Jim McDaniel that the last chapter of Virginia's beautiful life — her death and funeral service — has been committed to paper. His letter to me, written three weeks after Virginia's death, serves as a fitting epilogue to this volume. Although I never had the opportunity to meet Jim, I owe him a huge debt of gratitude for the service he has done us all by sharing with us an account of his friendship with Virginia, an account that, coincidentally, documents Virginia's final days.

I have been engaged in the process of bringing these pages to publication for more than four years now, and many debts have been incurred along the way. I am most grateful to all who have supported and encouraged me in this project: my wife, Ellie, who, although she never met Virginia, knew how important this project was to me; my sister, Mary, whose advice and moral support have been invaluable; my sister, Kathryn, who is one of Virginia's biggest fans; Father Keith Hosey, Julie Barrett, and Jean Black, longtime friends of Virginia's, who helped fill in some of the gaps in my knowledge with documents, pictures, and recollections; Mike Dubruiel of Our Sunday Visitor, who first recognized the merits of Virginia's journals and pushed for their publication; and family members, colleagues, friends, and even strangers who first learned of Virginia from my Web site, who throughout the years have offered encouragement when my spirit was willing but the flesh was too weak.

one

FEBRUARY 26, 1962, TO SEPTEMBER 4, 1962

*V*irginia went to high school at St. Joseph's Academy (SJA) in Tipton, Indiana, from 1956 to 1960. She continued to live at SJA for two years after her graduation, serving in various clerical capacities. Her "Letters" began in February of the second of those two years. The first volume of her "Letters" covers the remainder of that semester at SJA, her vain attempts to join various religious communities, the summer she spent with the Tanzilli family in Elwood, Indiana — her one and only experience of life outside of an institution — and her search for a new place to live the following fall. During her stay with the Tanzillis, she associates with a group of individuals who belong to a secular religious fraternity modeled upon the ideals and spirituality of Charles de Foucauld, hence her frequent reference to the "Charlies." She renews her vows on August 15, and feels drawn to commit her life to supporting the ministry of Father Keith Hosey as his co-missionary. She writes, "Queen of the World, smile upon even this wretched soul and teach it the art of Loving God, of serving Him continually, of knowing that whatever may happen is for the honor of Him and the good of my poor soul."

A.J.P.M.
[*Ad Jesum per Mariam* — "To Jesus through Mary"]

Monday, February 26, 1962

Dearest Mother, You might think that this is a new wrinkle, but it's not. It's a new diary. There are no appearances to that effect, but I felt that this might bring me closer to you and your Son, so I asked Daddy to get it today. I know you're kept so very busy all day, what with all the pleadings of your children, so I thought that after you get them pretty well settled for the night, I might come to sit at your feet, to tell you about all the thrilling experiences God had given me during the day, to confess how very ungrateful I have been and to seek your advice on how to do better. Please tolerate my childish prattle, smile upon my little anxieties, adjust the little crosses when I fail to dispose myself to their graces, and as my eyes close with the sweetness of your lullaby, turn my wandering thoughts heavenward to my heart's desire. And may the incessant beating of your Immaculate Heart bring to life in my soul that same love that brought upon you the motherhood of God and of us, the LOVE OF MY BELOVED, the love of your Son, Jesus.

This was Daddy's Day, God love him. He has been so persistent in trying to get a job with the State. These night hours are hurting him. Please reward his beautiful trust in Divine Providence soon. He was here for an hour-and-a-half this afternoon. It is wonderful seeing him so often, but then I think that he must be a very lonely man. I know that he relies even more than he thinks on me to elevate this suffering. Please make me a worthy daughter. And yet, when a convent is mentioned, a cloud seems to appear on his face. If I should go to wed your Son one of these days, as may perhaps be, please take care of him, love him dearly, and lead him gently over the steep paths.

A postcard arrived today from your faithful servant Father Munro. He reminded me of your cry of abandonment: "*Fiat mihi secundum verbum tuum!*" (Let it be to me according to your word). Teach it to me, not in lip service, but let it be imprinted indelibly upon my heart.

Tuesday, February 27

Please obtain for me the graces to accomplish what God asks of me. Take my weakness and give me His strength! By the way, God made characters like me, too, and though He really has no need for me, I'm sure that He has created one and He will lead me to it in His own good time. Please stay with me, Mother dear. I can't do anything alone! But "in Him I can do all things" which He asks of me.

Monday, March 5

Mrs. Ryan gave me the little deposit book today, and that thirty dollars looked mighty good on its pages. I hope to save as much as possible to get a dowry built up again. Not that I'm sorry for having used the hundred dollars from graduation to see Mama last summer. I shall never be sorry for that, although at times my heart ached to see her in such a weak condition, and even more to be asked to leave when only half the stay had terminated. I went there for only one reason, to tell her how very much I love her and pray for her. I cannot separate those two, for one supplements the other. However, I do feel that this savings account will be of help to Daddy should I enter a congregation in the near future.

Please tell me if I am being presumptuous in saying that I shall enter a convent. I desire that your *fiat* be ever on my lips, but I firmly believe that God is sending me to a convent sooner or later. And even if it should be later, please ask for me the grace to do anything He appoints — joyfully, with much LOVE of Him.

Saturday, March 10

Today has been a rather active one for me in my old age, but I rather enjoyed it. I gave our room a thorough cleaning this morning, then attacked my wheelchair, Viv-Ed. He, she, or rather it was mighty dirty from the weather we've had recently. Then I spent a most enjoyable hour with our Eucharistic Lord. I brought along MY BELOVED, a book I have wanted to read for a long time, but the light was too dim so I closed it after the first chapter. But that was sufficient to get my trend of thought on the cloister, and I just stayed there trying to talk it out with Him. After all, the decision isn't mine, but the idea of this total giving is daily growing in me, and I am now anxious to know the reply of the Sister Adorers of the Precious Blood in Lafayette.

Sunday, March 11

The Mother-Daughter tea was held this afternoon in the girls' dining room, with the Juniors, Seniors, and their mothers attending. But because I didn't have a guest, I stayed in my room. I always feel a little moody on this annual occasion. It is one of those days on which my longing for Mama is very real to me. And so today, if I squeezed your hand extra tightly, it was because I was glad that you were there.

Tuesday, March 13

Saw Father Keith privately this evening. He received a reply from the Sister Adorers of the Precious Blood that the stairs and the diet require a "no" from them to handicapped girls. Also, the Sisters of Jesus Crucified in Devon said that to take someone in my condition is against their rule. I asked Father if he would consider writing to the Carmelites in Indianapolis. He will do that for me, but I shan't get any hopes built up, for I know that they are very austere from reading MY BELOVED. However, I've fallen in love with them since reading the Little Flower's autobiography. Meanwhile, I shall continue the novena to your faithful spouse, St. Joseph, asking only your *fiat* and the grace to see and accomplish God's Will.

Wednesday, March 14

Spoke to dear SME [*Sister Mary Eugenia*] this morning about a "deal," and she has agreed that for the rest of this month we shall trade intentions in our *Memorare* to St. Joseph; she'll pray for me and I'll pray for her. I think that's really neat. Of course, you know already that mine is to see and perform only the Holy Will of God. Lord, that I may see!

Wrote to Daddy this afternoon. I asked Daddy about something I got in today's mail from the Catholic Digest Book Club. It is an entire library of Catholic information, twenty books — two to a cover — for a mere six dollars and membership in the Club. How I would love to have these, for really the better we are steeped in the knowledge of God and His Church, the better we can LOVE so good a Master, so sacred a Spouse. Please help me twist Daddy's arm if you get around to it, and of course if He wants it. Let me be ever cautious to seek the Holy Will of God in all things.

Bishop Carberry arrived this evening. How I wish that I might speak for a few minutes with him. Perhaps I shall write and ask for a weekend appointment one of these days. Our bishop sat behind the girls this evening at Benediction. I was sitting at the back of our chapel and perhaps let out a sour note, for he turned completely around once when we were singing. If so, pardon me! I try, Mother, to tell you I love you, even if I croak in doing so.

Thursday, March 15

Well, Mother, I have yet to get packed for the weekend with the Certains. How I love that great family! I always anticipate visiting them, sharing the beautiful family life that is theirs, that must have been yours also with Jesus and Joseph at Nazareth. That's the "Charlie" coming out in me again. I long for Nazareth!

Monday, March 19 (Feast of St. Joseph)

It was wonderful for me to be with "my own family" again. Mary and I had a great time and many giggles together. We returned home shortly before five this evening. It was the first time I actually cried after saying goodbye to them.

This Wednesday is the day of recollection for the women of the Muncie deanery. I'm praying that I might attend, for Julie Barrett has offered to be my "feet" for the day. I shall see Mother Gerard about it tomorrow.

Well, Mother dear, I must prepare for bed. Besides, you must be weary at all this small talk. Just know that I love you and HIM, that I have missed the solitude necessary to speak to you as often as I would have wished this weekend, and although I didn't always get to complete the Holy Office, I wish to offer the joy and peace I knew with that wonderful family as a prayer. Smile on them sweetly, Mother, for I love them as my own. Reward them for their generosity to me and tell Him how I've enjoyed having my very own family for three days. Thank you, Mother dear, for being so understanding and patient with me. You know the pain I have suffered as a result of our family's separation from me, and especially from God. Please unite us in eternity, in HIM.

Tuesday, March 20

With Mary Ellen Kelly I rejoiced at the dawn today. I welcomed the routine, the tremendous treasures of Holy Mass and Communion, the time for private prayer and the Holy Office throughout the day. Let me remain always near Him! That is my only request, Mother dear. I never wish to be separated from my Eucharistic Spouse.

Saw Mother Gerard this evening, and she gave me permission to go to the Day of Recollection here tomorrow for the women of the Muncie deanery. I was so very glad, and will be assured of "feet" all day with Julie behind me. Bless that grand friend!

Wednesday, March 21

First of all, please tell Him thanks for a wonderful day for me. Mother, everything was great, and I do feel that I may claim Julie's "spoiled" medal this evening. Julie had two "Charlie" friends with her, Velma and Mary Joan. They're both tops, and I am proud to have had the opportunity to know them a little better, for I feel that even I may call them sisters.

Julie had brought her relic of St. Thérèse, and I got to hold it most of the day. It was a reminder of the "Little Way" I wish to imitate. I am so happy that I have finally come to value the Little Flower's friendship so much more than even before. I told Julie that I thought the relic was Thérèse's corn, and she repeated the comment when she and Velma were seated behind

Virginia and Velma meet for the first time

me in chapel. You can guess which of your spoiled brats got the giggles, but then I thought I saw a faint smile on your lips, so I didn't feel too bad.

Friday, March 23

This afternoon, I finally got around to writing a long letter to Sister Roberta. It amounted to four typewritten pages, for I went into extensive detail about my physical condition, etc. I asked Sister to further the information to the right channels for me. Mother, show us!

I also answered the bunch of letters that Sister Marie Josine brought from her class. In my letter to the children I tried to introduce myself and my handicap, and my happiness with it. Perhaps I may give them a few insights into the happiness of suffering, and the feelings of the handicapped. This is a good little apostolate I've started, and I beg the grace to glorify God — and not myself — through it.

Please thank Him for the little cross I received this evening. I thought the stave poking me last night was a little difficult, but now one of the hip paddings is off and the steel is digging the flesh at that particular point. Take even this to Him, Mother, and tell Him I Love Him alone. Thanks be to God!

Saturday, March 24 (Feast of St. Gabriel)

Got our room cleaned, and that was about all I accomplished today. This fatigue is quite a handicap at times. Did He make that, too? Of course I know He did, and He must have felt it many times, especially on the road to Calvary. So this is just another opportunity of learning Christ. Teach me, Mother!

This afternoon I phoned Daddy about the back brace. He said that he will take it with him to Indianapolis when he goes Monday.

The March issue of LIFE IN THE FOLD arrived today. It is, as always, of great interest to me. Am hoping to hear from Mère Michelle soon with hot news from France. Of course, I realize that the important thing right now for me is patience. And what better time to learn than during the sacred Lenten season, from the suffering, patient, loving Christ? Passion of Christ, strengthen me!

Sunday, March 25 (Feast of the Annunciation)

Happy Feast day, Mother! And a happy, happy one you have made it for me. I really don't know how to thank you for it, so I'll just say that I love you dearly. That says everything. Love.

Don't really know where to begin. Holy Mass was more beautiful than ever this morning. I could well imagine your joy when He came again, this time in a little white host, waiting for us to say *fiat* so that He might dwell within our hearts. Precious hope. God is with us!

I was chatting in Sister Eugenia's office after Benediction this afternoon when someone said that Julie was downstairs. But by the time I got out of the office, she had been to our room and come after me. With her was Velma Tanzilli, one of the "Charlies" that attended our day of recollection last Wednesday.

It was such a pleasure to see them again, and we went to my room for what I thought would be another of those ever-Loving discussion periods, but was I ever fooled! We giggled a little while about the ad I cut from last week's Time magazine. I had it lying on my bookcase and Julie noticed it when she came here the first time looking for me. It was an automobile advertisement that read: ALWAYS HAVE AT LEAST ONE FIAT, the ad *du jour*.

Julie asked me many times what I had said to St. Thérèse when I got to hold her relic last Wednesday. I had spoken of so many things to our dear Little Flower that I couldn't be specific in a reply.

Finally, Velma put her arm around me and asked me if I would consider living with her this summer, and I asked her to repeat herself. It was such a shock, and the remaining coaxings were too good to be true. I'd be living with the "Charlies," for her husband, Leo, belongs to the men's fraternity. I might even attend daily Mass. She showed me pictures of her husband, her two girls and their lovely home. Julie mentioned that two months ago Velma was cleaning out a little back room, wondering what she would use it for. She said that now she knows. I found it almost too wonderful to believe, and when I saw that it was really true, I could only hug her and cry. I told her that I have little to offer but my love and prayers. She will accept these and told me that she really needs me. I was never told before that I was needed. Mother, it is truly a good feeling, for somehow I believed her. Although I know so very little about her, I love her so much. Of course, I could give no answer till I spoke with Daddy this afternoon.

Daddy came about four. I mentioned the events of the afternoon to him soon after his arrival, and we discussed the plans during the visit. Everything is A-OK! I am thrilled. Mother, I could go on and on, telling you of so very much that has filled my heart to the brim with happiness, but the hour is late and I must retire. *Deo gratias*!

Monday, March 26

After Rosary last night, Sister Eugenia came down to see what I was all a-tingle about. I had mentioned that I had news, but it must wait till I had consulted Daddy. Well, I nearly burst, but I kept it secret all day. She rejoiced with me, understanding as she does just how much this will mean to me, and what a grand family life I shall participate in. Jesus, Mary, Joseph, I love you!

The events of the day were certainly not conducive to sleep, and the absence of the bumpers [*back brace*] even less so. So two to four were the only hours I really rested. It really showed today, for I wasn't much count. Little do we realize just how important our rest is until we're denied it. I just played Myriam's "My Fair Lady" soundtrack and let the happiness perk. *Deo gratias*! Never let me forget to thank Him for all things, such joys as He has lavished upon me, and the opportunities to follow this Way of the Cross, His way home.

Tuesday, March 27

The hour is the latest I have ever tried to write you, 10:45, so it must be a quickie. But so very much has happened that I couldn't possibly leave this go tonight.

Mother Landri will have me to Regina Mundi for a week's retreat. In other words, they are reconsidering. The main objections seem to be the perpetual motion and a speech defect which they think would keep me from singing the Holy Office. We'll show them! This is all I ask, a chance to show them just what I can do.

And now I must prepare for bed, happy in the thought of a pending engagement, something I hold sacred, and unworthy as I am, I beg your help in teaching me to serve my Beloved.

Friday, March 30

Mother, I am so eagerly anticipating the trip. I realize that my chances are slim, that they might feel they cannot take me, or I might feel that I don't belong, but I do know that a week's retreat will certainly be a boon to my Lent, and I beg you to stay always at my side, telling me never to lose sight of your Son and His Holy Will. Dear Mother, I need some very special care this week. And I love you. Queen of the World, smile upon even this wretched soul and teach it the art of Loving God, of serving Him continually, of knowing that whatever may happen is for the honor of Him and the good of my poor soul.

Sunday, April 8

It has been so very long since I last wrote, but it was even nicer to keep in touch, person to person, during the eight-day retreat at Regina Mundi Priory. Thank you, my Mother dear, for such a wonderful opportunity.

The time went very quickly, for our days were very well filled with prayer and work, as true Benedictines. The days were very well arranged and served to grant me much rest, which I needed so badly. And I can truly say that I felt much better because of it.

Mother Landri came to my room Tuesday evening, and it was then that I asked her if I might stay and again received a negative answer, with insistence that my vocation is to be a secular oblate. I was given the book of rules for the Oblature then. Thursday Mother spoke to me more thoroughly on the oblates, and she also suggested that she might be able to place me in that area to work in one of the institutes for my room and board and to be near the Sisters always. I told her how I loved the Sisters, but I was still undecided and wished to speak with Father Keith before giving her any definite answer. She also came in this morning to bid me farewell, permitting me to take the book of rules with me to show Father. And I kissed her goodbye after the None prayer, telling her I'd let her know my decision soon.

On the way home from Indianapolis, it took only a few words from Father Keith to clear up a very confusing situation for me. He simply said that if I am to be an oblate I may belong to the Charles de Foucauld organization, which is close to here in his parish. I admitted that this is how I felt about it but that I didn't know God's Will for me, which is all that really counts. Father said that unless God shows us otherwise, He is leading us on the path of our choice. And now, Mother, I have decided that this is the thing to do. I must write to Mother Landri, and though I love her and the others so, I must explain the reasons why I do not choose to be an Oblate of the Sisters of Jesus Crucified. Help me please, my precious Mother, to see and accomplish only His Will, completely ignoring the "objects of our desires" as St. John of the Cross has said. *Fiat!*

Tuesday, April 10

I wrote letters to Velma and Julie today, then went down rather early to make a visit before Confessions. Before Father Keith entered the confessional he told me that the "Charlie" priest from Canada, Father LeClerc, would see me after he had completed his office. When he left chapel, I followed, and we went to chat in the art room. It wasn't long till Father Keith joined us, and we had a beautiful conversation about "Charlie." I am very happy, Mother dear, that I got to meet this great priest, prospective superior of Father Keith, and that he gave me a special mission to be performed just for "Charlie." I am to back Father Keith with my prayers and sacrifices, and I am so happy because now I feel that I, too, can take part in this tremendous movement. I believe that the prospects are illimitable for the future, and I beg your aid for all those who are striving to live the ideals of Brother Charles of Jesus. Please be their Loving Mother.

Before I bade Father Keith farewell, he asked me if I planned to renew my vows this Easter. I have anxiously anticipated that great day, and Father said that he'd try to find someone to bring me a copy of *Seeds In The Desert* so that I may reread the chapters on Poverty, Chastity, Love, and Obedience. Hope that someone is Julie or Velma, for I always anticipate their visits.

Goodnight now, my Mother dear. Please grant that I may one day have even a "Charlie" heart, filled to the brim with Love and surmounted by the Cross of my Beloved, the Cross that I beg to carry worthily.

Friday, April 13

Mother, before I go to bed, let me kiss your maternal lips and tell you how grateful for your Tender Loving Care I am. And although in today's Liturgy you stand there suffering with your Son, you still caress me tenderly as He proclaims all of us your true children. Let me also, even in intense suffering, turn my concerns to those around me and Love them because Christ is there.

Sunday, April 15

Mother, everything was wonderful today. Thank you for your care in bringing this all about, for you do know just what we need. And you know how I need the Tanzillis. They took me from Church to their lovely home, or may I say OUR lovely home? Mother, it's beautiful. It wasn't built for a wheelchair and there are some pretty tight squeezes, but we'll get things worked out fine. Leo plans to build a ramp to get me on the porch from the sidewalk.

We had a nice breakfast and afterwards chatted a little while. How I love all of them! The girls, LuAnn and Carolyn, are darling and couldn't stop showering me with love and kisses. Such a beautiful family I have. Help me to give myself to them as they have given this happiness to me.

Well, Mother dear, I am so very tired today. Right now the record player is playing "I Could Have Danced All Night" into my happy Dumbo ears, and I think I *could* dance, the way I feel. My heart is dancing with Him. But I must get ready for all the things in store in Dreamland. The Tanzillis are probably waiting there already. But first, please accept this goodnight kiss from a very tired and happy child. I LOVE you!

Monday, April 16

Please bestow from your treasure house of all God's graces those in which I'm most in need now. Let me no longer value others' opinions as highly as I have in the past. Let me seek only God's Will in all things and let nothing else matter. The servant certainly isn't better than the Master. When I gaze upon His suffering frame, I see that there is no bitterness from which I must desire exemption. I embrace this also, for a "Charlie" heart must love in the shadow of the Cross.

Tuesday, April 17

Father encouraged us to make a little retreat, as much as possible, during these days commemorating the passion and death of our Beloved. No other days of the year provide such opportunities for our spiritual growth. But first the seed must DIE. Mother, help me! Fill this poor little "Charlie" heart with *Caritas*, and let it grow up in the shadow of the Cross.

Spoke with Father after supper. I shall renew the vows of Poverty, Chastity and Obedience at the Easter vigil! Father Keith will be the celebrant. Mother, help me to give my all, every weakness that keeps me from complete abandonment. Just let me be your little one, and since I no longer possess anything of this world, help me to find at last everything in my Spouse.

Wednesday, April 25

Such a merry-go-round I've been on this past week, dear Mother! Have I taken time out to tell you how I love you? Guess I could never forget that, and yet if I don't say it you know it, don't you? Yes, I love you in your suffering and your joy in the cycle we have just begun; I love you now and I'll always love you because you're my Mother. *Deo gratias*!

Most of Holy Saturday was spent in preparation for the big events of that night. *Seeds In The Desert* proved a booster for me, especially the chapters on Poverty, Chastity, Love, and Obedience. And then, before we knew it, the time had come for the beautiful Easter Vigil. At the Offertory, I could do nothing but let my hands extend as a sign of the complete consecration I was making to my Beloved in the light of renewing the three vows that I had taken for the first time last December 8. What a JOY it is to have nothing, yet possess all things!

Thursday, April 26

This afternoon I had quite a long nap after Office and Rosary. The heat shortened it somewhat, and I can see that these bumpers are going to be really "good for me" this summer. Mine to give? Not really, but mine to thank Him for.

Sunday, April 29

I went to Mass with the Tanzillis this morning. When we arrived, the First Communicants had just filed into their pews and were singing a hymn. It gave me opportunity to remember that day of days in my life, when Christ came to me for the first time. Help me to be as pleasing to Him as I was that day, to let no stain mar His beauty in me.

It was difficult to leave home this afternoon, but that too is "good for me." Julie came with Velma and me to the Motherhouse. But a flood broke out in my room when I said goodbye to Velma. How beautiful are friendships, and how I love all with whom I come in contact!

Monday, April 30

Sent Velma a card today. Yes, it is a painful yet grand feeling to be homesick.

Friday, May 3

It was simply impossible to write last night, and even now the hour is very late. However, I feel this need to communicate this to you in these silly but sincere letters. My confidence that you will read them, silly as they may seem, and that you will give your poor little one all she needs to learn to LOVE, knows no bounds, *Car vous êtes ma mère!*

Saturday, May 4

Today was a mighty rough one, Mother. And I am most grateful for all the special little pushes you gave me. I know not where this excessive fatigue and pain come from, but I pray that you might show me all the opportunities that come with them. Show me how the Divine Lover acted under these circumstances and I, too, unconditioned as I am to pray worthily during such periods, will simply delight to remain in the silence and love of His Sacred Heart.

Thursday, May 10 [Her twentieth birthday]

Saw Father Keith after Mass and got to go to Confession. Instructions: Begin on these next twenty years. They're important! Yes, Mother, every precious little second is important. But how can a poor little child like me use them as I should? I can't! Mother, please, I need your guidance. But with you with me I can do whatever my Beloved desires to do with me. "Set thyself as a seal upon my heart, that in thee and through thee I may be found faithful to God." Yes, this is the third anniversary of my Total Consecration to you. I am your slave, but most of all I am your little child. You are my Mother, and I LOVE you.

Saturday, May 12

Tonight is a difficult one for me. It was precisely one year ago that I sat in Stinky's [*a classmate*] arms and sobbed my heart out for a mother that wasn't there for me to heap my love on that Mother's Day. What an empty feeling overcomes me this time of the year, and how I long to tell Mama how I love her! Please tell her for me, my Mother.

Monday, May 14

I wanted so badly to get my hair washed and set this evening, but there was no one who would do it. Guess they were too excited about the *palladiums* that came today and look much better loaded with autographs. It is so difficult to find anyone to assist me at this stage. Please give me the humility to keep asking and to keep blessing even the negative responses. This is so very hard for your weak little child. Teach me, Mother, your beautiful humility.

Wednesday, May 16

Received a letter today from Mother Michael. It is always such a pleasure to hear from her. There is no news at present. Same advice, be patient. Mother, will your poor little child ever learn this lesson? Please teach me. I shall try much harder to heed this lesson. Forgive me for all my failures in this practice and let me find this gem also to study in your crown.

Thursday, May 24

Yesterday Myriam and I took a walk to pray the Rosary at your Fátima shrine, and I lost the little white rosary that is such a favorite of mine. Please help me find it, Mother. Many are the times you and I have spent together with it, and I guess you might say I have a sentimental attachment to it. If this attachment is too great, however, it is good that I lost it.

Tuesday, May 29

Today was a very busy day, what with office work and cleaning my room. But finally the long-awaited moment came, and there was Julie to take me HOME. What a happy moment. We loaded Uncle George and were off, literally.

What a grand feeling: home for real. HOME: what a beautiful word, and thank you, Mother, for helping me to broaden my vocabulary to such a beautiful extent.

Thursday, May 31

What a beautiful "Charlie" day this has been. The Feast of the Ascension and also of your Queenship. Mary, my Queen and my Mother, remember that I am yours. Keep me and guard me as your property and possession! Let me realize that He has gone to His Father so that He might come to me in a much more intimate union than He came to you at the Annunciation. Let me hold Him as you held Him in every Communion that passed your sweet lips. Let me realize that He is giving Himself to me, to be with me always, to act not upon me but in and through me. Let me not search the sky till I can no longer find Him here within. Let Him become more and more real to me. Pray for me, Mother!

Monday, June 4

At Mass this morning Pat gave me the Litany of Humility which I've wanted ever since I saw it in Julie's missal. Now, Mother, here's another request from your little one. I know that I ask for so very many things, but I have no one to turn to but you, whom I love so much. If I should ask for anything that I may not have, help me to utter your *fiat* without trying to reason it out. Yes, even in this request, that I might learn meekness and humility. What Father Keith told me the other day about confidence certainly applies to this, also. Can I learn to desire to have even a poverty of these virtues, of clinging entirely to Him, desiring not even the possession of humility or confidence except what He wishes to give me? I can, but only with your help. Please, Mother, I need you to help me to empty myself entirely so that, like you, I may bear Christ.

Monday, June 11

This was a really "off" day, and I do owe my Beloved many, many apologies. Will you please tell my Love of the sorrow that fills my heart and beg His graces and forgiveness for me?

For one thing, Daddy took the brace last night to have it fixed in Indianapolis and didn't return with it till late this afternoon. The pain was quite violent at times, but I fear that I complained much too much. Teach me to suffer alone, and to be happy with everything because I go with God. Let me not diffuse misery, but CHRIST.

Also, Daddy asked me to let Jimmy have our record player for the summer. My vow of poverty seemed to vanish, and I begged to be permitted to keep it for myself. It wasn't just that I had saved all last summer to get it, but also Mama gave me the rest of the money I needed to buy it, so that I consider it something she has bought for me. And since it is the only thing that I have which she gave me, it means very much to me, too much as I see by my conduct this afternoon. Although I gave it to Daddy, it wasn't with a very willing heart. Teach me detachment!

Saturday, June 16

Mother, take this little heap of burned-out incense. This is all I have to offer today. Of great works or profound prayers I was bereft. But here I lay, a wretched sight, and this is my all for God today. The miserable pain continually gnawing at my back and neck would have been unbearable, had you not sustained me. Thank you, Mother. All the tasks I began collapsed, and I lay at God's feet, only pain and complete happiness. *Deo gratias!*

Thursday, June 28

For some reason or other today has been rather difficult. Velma and I were talking this morning, she telling me that she and Leo will take me to Owensboro [*Kentucky*] next month to see my precious Sisters of the Lamb of God. Wouldn't that be great? I love all the Sisters so much and treasure the moments spent at Our Lady of Hope. But then I noticed the calendar and the fact that I shall be spending only a month and a half more here at home. Now, I know that this is utterly ridiculous and very ungrateful on my part to be feeling this way, and I keep telling myself that. But no matter what I say, nothing makes me happy at the prospect of returning to SJA this fall. Perhaps that isn't what bothers me most. It's the fact of leaving this beautiful family and all my "Charlie" friends in Elwood, only twelve miles distant, yet so very far away that I shan't be able to attend even the meetings of the "Charlies." O sure, I did last year for two times, but the Sisters really were against those long weekends. Mother, this is a tremendous request, and yet you who are the treasure house of all God's gifts can surely give it if it be His Holy Will. Ask your divine Son to permit me to stay here even this winter. Please! Yet not my will but His is important. And so I fling myself into your loving arms with boundless confidence and beg you to let me always stay there. I know that you will bring me to where I can best love Him. And no more must I ask, no more do I ask. Only LOVE.

Saturday, June 30

Julie came for a little while this afternoon. She has had her purse stocked for a month with cigars from the new aunt, so I took one, a pink one, and chewed it all afternoon. It was bubble gum, and I feel fine. Don't think I got cancer. But I am trying to get attention with some serious illness. Got a bad heat rash from the back brace and it seems to be infected. We're trying to diagnose it as leprosy, so I might get sent away any day. That would be a grand apostolate, but I'd miss our "Charlie" terribly. Guess I like sticking around here after all. If you are wondering about me, well you have a right. But I still love you, so I'll make it.

Sunday, July 1 (Feast of the Precious Blood)

Leo, the girls, and I attended the ten o'clock Mass. In the homily, Father Keith delved into a beautiful consideration of our excuses for not being a saint. They look pretty shallow when Father presents them, but when I try to rid myself of them I find them very difficult to conquer. Why am I not a saint NOW? Mother, I CAN be, with your help. But without you I am doomed to failure. Yet I know that you shan't permit this if I but prostrate myself at your feet and beg to be taught the lessons you taught your divine Son. I have not done this often enough, but now I begin again. Mother, dry my tears, ignore my wretchedness, and help me learn Christ.

After Mass I discussed with Father Keith my taking the trip to Chicago this July 4th. I know it's a long drive and would probably be very hard on me, but how I desire to meet the Little Sisters, to see their way of life so that I might better imitate it. The thing that drew me back was not the difficulty of the long drive that Father was concerned about, but getting up the four flights of rickety stairs in orders to reach the Little Sisters' apartment. So now I wait, desiring this trip very much, yet listening for the whisper to which I must say *fiat*.

Wednesday, July 4

Please, Mother, forgive me for all the childish pranks I've pulled today. Velma and I were just going out the door to Holy Mass this morning when the phone rang. And it kept ringing till, lo and behold, Velma found out that she was going to Chicago after all. This whole trip has been so mixed up it's turned into a comedy. So she gulped down her breakfast, Father Keith got a nurse for Grandma, and they were off, just like that. But I gave the group a horrible sendoff. You see, I hadn't given up hope of going myself, silly though it was. So when Father walked in the door with the others, I burst out crying. I had tried so very hard to keep it back until they were gone, but I had reached the breaking point. How I wanted to dry off and tell Velma how happy I was that she and the others were going, to send a little message to our dear Little Sisters, to smile and say that since I was unable to make such a long trip I would certainly be with them in spirit, but I could say nothing, not even good-bye.

How very much I've missed Velma today. Mother, it scares me to think of leaving her and the "Charlies" this fall. *Fiat, fiat, fiat*! When shall I learn? Please help this stupid child.

Thursday, July 5

It was such a treat to see Velma this morning. I just couldn't hug her enough or finish telling her how I had missed her. And, of course, I was all ears to hear about the trip. They had six hours with the Little Sisters, and had a grand time, which isn't surprising, considering the company. Velma brought out a huge sucker, about twelve inches in diameter. Father Keith had bought it for me on their way home. Nothing could have meant more to me than to know that I was truly thought of, even with all those beautiful souls surrounding him. Although he bought it probably as a compliment to simplicity, I knew that God was showing me something else. That sucker told me how very far this little baby must go to reach the true childlike simplicity for which I must continue to strive. It showed me that I needed much sweetening to be a suitable morsel for the Christ Child. Mother, teach me to truly be your little one, to prove my love for you.

Friday, July 6

Velma and I discussed my feelings about returning to Tipton this fall. I try to say *fiat*, Mother, but it still hurts to think about it. I just don't know how I'm supposed to feel. But then, if I want His Will above all else, even if His Will hurts me at times, is this not right? Mother, please teach me the abandonment which I so lack. Will I ever reach the point where His Will and mine are one? If so, what might I suffer for my Beloved to prove my love? Please teach me just what I should be doing in this regard.

Please help me profit by the many mistakes I make every day, and obtain for me the grace of an inexhaustible effort in following Christ each day, a step at a time.

Saturday, July 7

Today I began that very powerful novena to St. Joseph. What is the request? That I might learn to pronounce your *fiat*. Mother,

I haven't even begun, and I fear that even a lifetime will find me not much further. But nothing is impossible in the inexhaustible love of God, and there is my only hope, and entire assurance. Help this little one who has cast herself at the feet of her Mother. I can barely lisp it now, let alone realize the full significance of what I'm trying to say. Only when I have been saturated with the LOVE of God can I begin this death. But I have a Father Who loves me and a Mother who is always guiding me to Him, and I am blind if I cannot rejoice in all this.

I went to Confession this afternoon. Father Keith had some alarming news, however. He had been to Tipton recently and talked to a couple Sisters concerning me. Although Mother Gerard would never let me down, the others feel that I no longer belong there. I have become too burdensome to the Sisters and the girls, and also I cannot keep the tight schedule that I must if I work there. Father suggests that I look elsewhere for some place to live. He even asked if the deal at Good Samaritan in Kokomo still holds. Mother, do you really think that I am to be in an old people's home? Ah yes, love is certainly in demand there as much if not more than elsewhere. But I know not what to think about it. Also Father said that perhaps my trip to Owensboro this month will bring something for me. Please tell me where God wants me, what He wishes of me! All this is so very hard to swallow. Do I really belong anywhere? Let me make my abode in the Sacred Heart of Jesus. Then will I begin to love as I should.

For my penance I was told to go home and not to worry. Teach me the complete abandonment needed to accomplish this, and let me live each precious moment here with my family and never forget to thank my Father for it.

Tuesday, July 10

As Velma and I sat after dinner this evening, tears came to my eyes and a pang to my heart as I thought of leaving home, of leaving this "Charlie" who has become such a part of me. I do love her, Mother, and although I try not to care, to be completely abandoned to our separation, I do care. Mother, you who knew the tremendous pang of bidding your divine Son farewell, and then of holding His limp cold body at the foot of the Cross, give me the courage to do as He wishes, and nothing else. I love Him! Help me to prove it.

Friday, July 13

We gave Sister Eugenia a whale of a present today for her feast day: Velma and I didn't speak to each other. It was so very hard for me, because it gave me even more to consider the blank future that lies ahead of me. Mother, I try so very hard to leave it to His Providence, but I just can't forget it like that. It keeps popping up, and although I know He is my Father and will most certainly care for His little one, I sometimes feel so lost as concerns His work for me that I simply must spill out all this pain that lies aching inside me. And I did this on Velma's shoulder this evening, only minutes ago. Thank God for "Charlie" shoulders to cry on! That helps so much.

Monday, July 16

At breakfast, Velma told me that after she had gone to church yesterday evening for a little visit she spoke to Leo concerning me while they were at dinner. He has definitely decided that I must not stay here after the first agreed time, that is, this fall. I know not the reasons, although there must be some very good ones. I do know that this is Holy Obedience. And I thank God for making it so clear. But now that I know the places where I may NOT stay, can't we find the other side of the picture? Mother, my heart aches so very much sometimes that I can feel a physical pain deep within. I have wanted so long to belong, and yet it seems that God never wishes me to cuddle in this security. *Fiat, fiat, fiat!* But please give me the strength to do what He wants, and please show me. I look to you, my mother, with boundless confidence, for nowhere else can I place my hope. Accept the tears of your poor little one. I have so far to go before I can prove I love Him above all else. Help me!

Sunday, July 22

What a WOW day this has been. Thank you, Mother, for giving your little one just the tonic she needed at this difficult period. It is so grand to see our Father Keith on the altar, and to hear his love notes from the pulpit again. He is really floating from that retreat he just had. Guess he has to wear a long cassock to make people think his feet are still on the ground, but I truly doubt that they are. He was terrifffff in the confessional last night. So very gentle, understanding me as only he could. He told me that a person in my condition, not only with a physical handicap but also almost what one might call an orphan, must possess to the fullest extent the virtue of HOPE. Yes, Mother, of course I know this, and I beg of you to ask that God lavish this precious gift upon me and that I might receive it.

Saturday, July 28

Father said that he had been to see Mother Gerard yesterday. He spoke to her about my problem, rather, challenge. Mother told him that she wants me to feel that St. Joseph's is truly my home. But she sees the difficulties that have arisen and thinks that my going to Good Samaritan would be an excellent setup. There I would find what I've always wanted wherever I go, my Beloved in the Holy Eucharist. Of course, this has been my plea ever since I was told that I ought to look for another place to stay. Also, both Mother Gerard and Father Keith think that my being there not only to do typing for Sister but also to visit, love, and bring happiness to those people who are so alone would be a grand apostolate for me. This must be

His Will for me, and so I join this weak *fiat* to yours and pray that I might be His little handmaid.

Sunday, August 5

Mother, my heart desires to burst into song so very many times a day. So if I do lots of this during the day please include it in this *Deo gratias,* which I wish to utter as long as I shall live, and on into eternity. (Hope my voice improves by then.)

Talked to Father Keith a little and hope to go to Confession after Mass tomorrow to prepare for my vows, which I'll renew August 15th. Please help me to give myself so completely to my Beloved that I have no more of MINE but only HIS life within me.

Wednesday, August 8

How tired and racked with pain I've been lately. It seems that every time I eat there is pain somewhere in my abdomen, either in my stomach or my colon. The pains in my back and neck are sharper than they've been for a long time, and today I kept getting cramps or something like that in my right biceps. Fatigue is plaguing me, and yet sleep is so very difficult to get. *Deo gratias!* Who am I that He should shower these blessings upon me? I am a weakling, but in Christ I can do all things He asks. May I never attempt to carry this alone. I can't. But may I let Christ do all these things WITH me.

Thursday, August 9

Just a little note to you this time, Mother dear. For in my heart is a song, a *Magnificat,* for such a tremendous day as He has lavished upon your little one. And, though this praise may sound very weak, please listen well and sing it for me yourself. I know that you shall do this for me, because you're my Mother!

Velma and I went to Holy Mass this morning, begging the Holy Spirit to use us in His talks to the group this evening. And I begged that He use even the efforts it took to get ready for Mass. Each movement was sheer agony, and because the pain was too intense last night to get much rest, such simple things mounted up to sheer exhaustion. And I sat before the altar and offered this useless heap to God, in your arms. Thank you for holding me so close that I was shaken by the vibrations of your Immaculate Heart as it sang its "love you's."

Velma thought it best that I do nothing but rest after breakfast this morning. And the entire day was simply an extension of my prayer from the Cross. The weakness was too much for study or reading, even too much for meditation or formal prayer. I hung there with my Beloved, completely helpless, and completely happy. Never have I experienced such complete joy. It was as if God wished nothing more from His child than to hold her in His arms. I snuggle here; I got to go Home for a day.

Father Keith was here this afternoon to see how well we had prepared for tonight. He even suggested that someone else take my place at the meeting, but I just couldn't let this happen. O Mother, how great is your beauty! And yet how little you are truly known. I just had to go to sing your praises this evening. And that is precisely what I did. Our group numbered nearly thirty and there I sat with the tremendous responsibility of speaking to them concerning humility. I knew that this was impossible for me. Therefore I sat limp and let only the words the Holy Spirit put there flow to those who sat there so intently without my knowing they were there. The room was empty, and I sat there alone and sang a song about you. And this song has been and will always be here within my happy heart. I shall never know what He told those others there, but I'll always remember the lessons He taught me from within. And as Father Keith, in all his saintly wisdom, so aptly put it, this may help many there tonight, but doubtless the instrument used will benefit most.

We then went to the church for Holy Hour of adoration. My Beloved and I, alone among so many. I said a little, told Him how I loved Him, how happy I was that this pain kept intruding into our conversation to remind me to say I love you again. He embraced me, kissed me, and the peace that enveloped us was like a cloud that bore us to a place where Love is the only reality.

Sunday, August 12

Velma and I were such goofs last night. Both of us were dead tired. We sat in the kitchen till midnight, laughing our heads off at anything that was said, no matter how serious. I was glad we stayed up together, for this insomnia is very difficult right now and with someone to talk to I could get my mind off the pain.

About two o'clock Grandma struck up a conversation with herself, and when she began calling Velma I crawled in to waken her but didn't have the heart. So I came back to our room and told poor Carolyn to tell her mother Grandma was calling. Then I got so very sick, and both my bowels and stomach began heaving. Got about three hours of sleep finally, but then I had to go heave some more. Was reading how St. Thérèse tried to fool God by smiling through her pain. But how did she do it with trouble at both ends? Think He might know what's going on no matter how much pretending.

Tuesday, August 14

I spoke with Father Keith today. I was so very happy to get this opportunity before I renew my vows at the Offertory of the Mass tomorrow morning. And I gave him the little crucifix he had brought me from the Holy Land last year. Christ has been telling me many things through this little instrument. This is only one of the many I've had on which the corpus refuses to stay, and I know that He wishes me to find my place there and suffer and love. May this spot never be taken from me! Also, it will not stay on the chain around my neck. No longer shall I put it there, but it will remain to cast its shadow on my heart. I embrace it, and I love this way! Father now has that crucifix to remind him that I wish to remain thereon for my little brother.

O Mother, might I not offer myself for this modern Christ? Might I not stand back in the crowds like you and do my part in His spreading of the Gospel? Never have I had such a compulsion to offer myself so completely for someone I love. And I do love him, Mother. He is Christ to me, his words, his giving of all he has, health, solitude; this is the saint of our time. I desire to follow him always, lost in the crowds who press in upon him, who need him so. Our Lady of the multitudes, teach me to follow and love thus.

Wednesday, August 15 (Feast of the Assumption)

Mother, I have flung myself upon my Beloved for the third time. I'm His. Please let it be entire. I begged that this little heap of incense would burn out its last speck of self and truly belong to God in Poverty, Chastity and Obedience; to be borne to the Trinity of Love in the hands of my Mother, whose love let not even death separate her from the God she had nourished. Hail, glorious Queen. Reign always over your little slaves! This wasn't like the other days on which I promised myself to Christ through the three vows. Today I felt a driving compulsion to do something I'd never dreamed of before. It seemed that the Holy Spirit almost pushed me to offer myself for the spread of the Gospel through the instrumentality of Father Keith. O what a joy to know that I must back such a saint in his work! *Deo gratias!* Please let me never forget this vocation in all that lies before me.

Thursday, August 16 (Feast of St. Joachim)

What a joy this first day of retreat has been! When I think there are seven to follow I get so shook (you know me and my subdued emotions, and feet) that I must just stick to the present and not try to understand just how God is going to lavish even more upon His little one.

For our three o'clock conference this afternoon our subject was "What is a Christian." It was mentioned that a Christian's lot is confusion. And this is explicitly portrayed in the life of Brother Charles. From his adolescence he was always seeking, never finding quite what he wanted. Even after his complete conversion, when he so spent himself in the love of the poor Tuaregs [*nomadic peoples of the Sahara Desert*], he yearned for at least one companion to assure him that his work would continue. But none was granted; he was never permitted even a glance at the tremendous following he would one day have. He died completely alone. "All my plans turn out to be mere bits of paper." O how valuable are those little scraps to us today!

How alike are "Charlie" and I here: always searching for the Holy Will of Our Father, and never really sure that we are performing it. It has always been this way for me; no doubt it always will. But this tremendous happiness that now fills me so that I find it necessary to kick, to laugh and sing, is this how He wishes me to shout the Gospel now? If so, I can truly say I'm fulfilling my vocation in that respect!

Friday, August 17

What a beautiful night I spent with Christ last night! More so because not even sleep dared to intrude upon the joy. Father Keith's relic of the True Cross, the one he received in Rome for his ordination, was lying on the table in the conference room all day for us to adore. I just couldn't imagine leaving such a thing there alone all night, so took I it to my room and knelt there with it held tightly to my heart. O Holy Cross of my Beloved, I shall never let You go! And I experienced intense joy, and pain. Anne-Marie came in about one o'clock. She was so very sympathetic, wishing to do something, whereas there was really nothing for me but to stay there with my aching body, and love. Then Eileen came in an hour later and wanted to help me into the bed. When I had convinced her that I wished to remain on the floor, she told me how welcome I was to be here with them on retreat. She was such a darling. So then God's little vagabond took a crawl to chapel, where I had the opportunity of kneeling before the Blessed Sacrament for the first time in seven years. It was such a joy to be there and know that love needs no words. When at last I had drained the last jewel from this suffering, sleep did come to let me awake a little later to another day of communion with Christ.

After supper tonight I got to take a walk with Susan. Our visit lasted way into the night, till one to be exact. I was so very glad to have someone to speak to. Nights are so very hard for me at times. So very many times I can't sleep, and the pain is too intense to do any real praying. Then it is that I must place myself on the Cross to suffer with my Beloved. Had Father's relic again THIS night, for he thought it very good that I didn't leave it in the other room all alone. I cling to it until the metal makes dents in my arms. How blissful is my lot, and I hold it so that this one earthly good will be taken from me only at the moment of death, at the moment I begin to live the eternity this brings.

Saturday, August 18

Velma was here for the first time for the afternoon conference. I pretended not to look at her much, but I've missed her so that I just couldn't keep my eyes off her. But I refused to let our eyes meet, fearful of the tears which were already forming there because of the tremendous void in being away from her for these three days, and of the hidden sword that keeps pricking its reminder that soon we shall be parted for good.

After the conference, Velma came to hug me before she left, and I could no longer contain this horrible flood that welled within my heart, but opened the gates on her shoulder. How I sobbed, continued to sob, and can still feel a terrible pang in my heart. Teach me to love! If not you, to whom shall I go to learn to love your Son? Please, Mother.

During our review of life we discussed the beautiful relationships we term friendships. Dorothy read a beautiful quote to us on being separated from a friend and how there is really no distance involved, but rather a new awareness of the proximity the loved one has to us. I must get that from her today and make a copy of it, for you know how very much I need to learn this lesson. Father Keith knows this, too, and I got poked in the ribs by beloved little brother while that was being read.

Mother, teach me this lesson, especially now that I'm getting ready to leave ALL the dearest friends I've ever had, our "Charlies"; all those to whom I've been able to open up all the doors so that my true self could be seen, those who have really understood my babbling, those who have given me so much love in spite of all my wretchedness, or perhaps because of it. And even the only spiritual director I've ever found, I shall leave him too very soon. But I know that my heavenly Father isn't going to take from me anything that I need to find Him. From the experience I've had of being separated again and again from those who are such a part of my heart, I know that I can do nothing but grow in the love that I seem to be leaving. As Dorothy put it so well this evening, a *fiat* without pain isn't really worth much. Yes, this parting must hurt me so that I may truly offer it to God, for these I love so much. O Mother, teach me to love!

Monday, August 20

As I sat waiting for Father to come in for our morning conference, terrible fatigue, pain, and tremendous joy overcame me. I sat there pressing Father Keith's relic of the Holy Cross to my heart with all the strength left in me. O the joy that is mine, and although I thought it impossible, it has increased since I became Father's co-missionary on your feast. But that's Our Father, always quite a few steps ahead of us when it comes to giving Him something. He literally showers kisses upon me in return. But here's a little secret. It's such fun being a spoiled little one. And thanks for making me just that.

And the conference, well, it was the most striking I've heard since retreat began. When I look over the notes I scribbled down, I see nothing to overwhelm me, and yet deep within I could feel the Holy Spirit working where words are expressionless and would only mislead me from the reality of what He accomplished during that conference.

Father spoke to us concerning poverty, and you well know how deficient I've been in putting this virtue into practice. Mother, show me yourself at Nazareth. I need no other lesson. Father Keith had used lollipops as an example of attachments in our lives, and he showed that just as a five-year-old has such a strong attachment to such things, so we, too, may be able to go to great extremes of poverty — because we have a closet full of lollipops to comfort us. We were to find the lollipops in our own lives and discuss them at our review this evening.

It was so cute to hear Anne-Marie trying to find out where her "lollipops" were. So I pulled a fast one with the cooperation of some of our "Charlies." When it came my turn to tell of the lollipops I had found in my closet, I pulled out the huge sucker Father Keith had brought me from his trip to see the Little Sisters in Chicago. Anne-Marie's eyes looked like saucers and everyone roared. I had found my lollipop, that was obvious.

Tuesday, August 21

When I told Father I had packed his crucifix to bring it on to Tipton for the Apostolic blessing at the end of retreat, he told me I might keep it till that time! Mother, help me to somehow repay him by my giving of myself as his co-missionary. It is amazing how this has changed things, enriched my cross beyond expression. To know that I might share in his work for Christ makes me cling even harder to the cross of my Beloved. O blessed Cross of Christ, my arms ache with clinging to you, and they spur me to get an even firmer grasp!

Wednesday, August 22
(Feast of Your Immaculate Heart)

Happy, happy feast day, Mother dear!! I love you and sing joyfully as each of your feasts comes once again into our love cycle. And today is the feast of your loving heart, that stainless masterpiece that flung its joyous song to God with each beat. Let me rest in your embrace so that I might put my head to your breast and hear that perfect rhythm, and pattern my love songs to yours, so that Christ may not hear the little croaks that escape my lips but smile at the lullaby of His own Mother.

Father Keith pushed me back to the Motherhouse at lunchtime. I've tried so very hard to have a private conference with Father during this retreat, but since that had been impossible till then, I was grateful for the little exchange we had then. Father asked about my health, for he has noticed how very tired I've looked lately. That's how he is, always looking out for others. He looks mighty tired himself. Is this what his new co-missionary is doing for him? Please let some of this pain be applied to giving him the strength he needs in bringing Christ to all these souls so hungry for the *Caritas* he brings.

After the evening conference, Father asked if I would like to go to Confession. At last I got to speak with him, and I learned that we hadn't done so sooner because he didn't know just what to say about being my missionary. God love him! He knows so well the full significance I've laid upon this new vocation to be his co-missionary. This is so very clear to me. When Father LeClerc was here, he told me that since my apostolate must be a limited one, I must back this great movement to the spirit of Brother Charles with my prayers. He has chosen me, and my role is that of sitting at His feet. I must never waste time by wishing for Martha's part. Mine is to sit there, and listen, and LOVE. After Father LeClerc had said this to me, he told me that he would give me a very special assignment for Brother Charles. He told me that I would back Father Keith in his tremendous apostolate. What a privilege! And I, who had prayed for him so much before, now tried to double these meager but sincere offerings for him, knowing that God our Father would accept their lowliness because you, my Mother, would embellish them with your riches before you took such things of poverty to the divine majesty of the King.

And then I told Father just how this had changed since the fifteenth. How, when he walked past me [*that day*] on his way to the confessional just a few minutes before the Offertory, and told me with a turn of his hand, but most obviously with the glance of his eyes, that he knew the importance of the step I was about to take, of offering myself once again in my Poverty, Chastity and Obedience; how in that very second something moved within me. The Holy Spirit had spoken, and He told me that here was my missionary. It was as if I had not listened to the entire message from Father LeClerc, and the Spirit of Christ Himself found it necessary to make known this vocation.

We spoke of leaving Elwood and how this is tearing my heart from me. I told Father of how I felt, of how very much it hurts to have a taste of this Nazareth and then to be driven from it. And yet deep within I know that this is Christ Whom I love in the "Charlies," just as it was He at the Villa, at St. John's, and at SJA. And each time I left Him in these places I found Him wherever I went. Mother, the intense physical and mental anguish I've been going through recently cannot shake the tremendous peace and joy that fills my heart to overflowing, so that I must laugh, sing, cry, love all those I see. O Christ, my Lord, my God, my ALL. Nothing can take me from YOU.

Mary, let me find your beautiful Son, ESPECIALLY in the most miserable heart.

Finally it was necessary to leave the confessional, for there were others waiting. Guess we could have stayed all night, but with our "prudence" we decided to call it quits. Bet he doesn't avoid me for so long the next time! And then I had to come to my room, to cry. So very many things I had bottled inside (and you know that to bottle ONE thing is next to impossible for me) just had to come out, so that I was washed clean in the Sacrament of Penance, and then these waters spilled from my eyes in a salty gesture of love.

Thursday, August 23

Got to see Father this afternoon right before supper. I was so very confused about where I am to go this fall. So I asked his reasons for preferring me to go to Kokomo. As usual, he came up with some mighty good ones, and I ended up agreeing with him. I can do nothing else when I speak to him, for to me it is Christ speaking to me. And I am His.

Father pointed out my need to communicate the love God has planted within my poor little "Charlie" heart. He thinks that I definitely belong at the Good Samaritan [*nursing home*] in Kokomo, where I might go to love all those who have been left there alone to suffer. What a tremendous apostolate, and the more I think of it the more I realize that this is His Will for me now. And so, the more I think of Father's words and of their value, coming from one with the wisdom of God, I can see that this IS what I must do. And with this assurance I run to it, to "shout" the Gospel, by my little life of love. Help me, Mother!

Saturday, August 25

Teach me to DESIRE MORE POVERTY, WANT, AND MISERY in this soft little way I've tried to create. Please forgive me for my constant striving for security. I should know by now that God doesn't wish me to have anything but uncertainty, so that I might gain all this AFTER I have earned it by a life of utter confusion and complete joy in knowing that this was the lot of the Infant Jesus. O that I might be called soon to dwell forever in the security of God's embrace, and yet I should not even express this yearning. Let me wait like Jesus, in the care of you, my Mother, and all those whose hearts burn with *Caritas*, happy to spend myself for others by letting them feed and clothe me. Teach me this poverty, Mother of the Infant Jesus, and my Mother. I place my complete confidence in your maternal care, for this is my one certainty. *Deo gratias*!

Sunday, August 26

I got to spend much time before my Beloved today, spilling myself entirely and begging that He now live and love within me. My Mother, remember that I am yours. Let my prayer mingle with yours, for how else might I present such a wretched gift to God? But because you are my Mother, you will take care of my failings and teach me to love as you do, with nothing but Jesus-Love. My God, hasten the day that I can learn this from Our Mother!

When I wasn't in chapel today, I spent all the rest of my time sleeping. It was so very good for me, and perhaps I shall gain a little strength with this rest I'm getting. This pain and exhaustion have left me very weak recently, and I pray that through this bit of suffering Father Keith may find the strength he needs to carry the nearly unbearable load he has shouldered. And because Our Father has been so kind as to let me do this little something so that I might somehow help Father Keith "shout" the Gospel in his saintly life, I beg that this be not taken from me, but that the strength to carry it and far greater sufferings be granted me. Help me, Mother. Only a weakling am I who begs this, but there is an inexhaustible source of strength in the Christ Who lives within me.

Monday, August 27

It is a very cozy, glowing feeling to be home at Nazareth once again. Did Christ stop in at His old home once in a while to bathe in His happy memories there? Did you fix His favorite meal and tell Him how you loved Him to be there? I think that you did, just as Velma did for me. I love her so and think that she must be very much like you at your home in the former Elwood called Nazareth.

Mother, this is very difficult for me never to have any security. And I'm so very weak. I cling to Father's Cross, and I know that even these sobs I cannot stifle are an acceptable offering for "my" missionary. *Deo gratias* that I have something to give for him today. How can I thank Him? Please take this heartache, this love, for him!

Tuesday, August 28 (Feast of St. Augustine)

Went to Holy Mass with Julie and Theresa this morning, on this feast of a great guy to whom Father Lucien introduced me last January in suggesting that I read his "Confessions." Bless that Father Lucien! When I see what tremendous results St. Monica's prayers and tears worked in her son, I receive the strength to continue entrusting my Mama's soul to the love and mercy of Our Father, knowing that these prayers and tears of mine for her will not be ignored.

When Julie took me to the foot of your altar after Mass, I could no longer contain my tears of confusion, my weaknesses, but just had to spill them at your feet, knowing that you would take even these bitter drops and make them a sweet offering to the Baby Jesus. Please tell Him that I need His strength now so that I might bear this, and much more, because I love Him. And thank you for letting Father Keith come to the communion rail just as we were leaving to remind me that this is all for Him. Thank you so very much! This makes all these silly little heartaches such big joys. Let me never forget my vocation as a co-missionary.

There were so very many things I wished to do today, but there was so little Christ wished of me. He kept trying to tell me that today was to be spent from the Cross. I tried to put a

Julie Barrett and her
daughter, Theresa

dent in the huge correspondence awaiting me, but found all the little arm movements quite painful, and holding my arms here to do typing is simply exhausting. So here I sit, trying to get my letter to you typed before I must let these silly arms drop from exhaustion. Even pressing Father's crucifix to my heart is painful, so I kneel on the floor, my arms straight at my side and my heart fixed upon the Sacred Wood that bore my Beloved before me. But now I am lying on that Cross, and beg that the Christ who has permitted me such a burden will accept this weakness I place there, for him, for Father Keith. Mother, give me your gentle arms in which to embrace my God.

Wednesday, August 29

After Mass, I handed Father my favorite card from the stack Velma had given me. There was a big bear on the front, with a little bear hanging on his leg and a heart above the little one's head. On the inside it read, "You're the most." Yes, our

Father Keith is the most, the most Christlike of all those beautiful souls God has strewn on this little path to Himself. Please teach me to be worthy of having known him and more especially of being his co-missionary for life. What a vocation! Thanks loads for planning it this way. And please teach me that I need never worry about the future, for I see this lovely and exciting pattern that keeps opening for me and know that its design will be completed finally in the Sacred Heart of Christ. Home at last!

Friday, August 31

Leo and I took a little jaunt through the streets tonight. How I love to pass the lighted windows of all the little homes, and I think the Holy Spirit wanted to tell me much. It was grand of Leo to suggest that walk, and wise as he is, I'm sure he was thinking of more than the stars and fresh air when he suggested it.

I peeked into all kinds of windows, saw families eating, talking, watching TV. And I wondered about their happiness, their love or security. There were so very many cozy little houses, but just how many homes did we pass? Are they as happy as I who hold Christ right here within my heart? Do they love and are they loved as is this little vagabond, who consumes the flames of divine Love each morning that they may burn bright within my heart throughout the day? Help me, vagabond that I am, to show them somehow where to find that for which they search.

Thank you, Mother, for all you taught me tonight. Please thank Leo for me. I love him so and wish that I might return something of what he has given me in accepting me into his Nazareth this summer. May this happy home continue in the ways of your Holy Family. Please keep these always for the God Who meant homes to be thus.

Tuesday, September 4

Here I knelt tonight and embraced Father's Cross, and cried bitter tears. And I was thankful to be alone at last and let these drops of sorrow and joy fall upon the same splinters that had received Christ's tears, and His Precious Blood. And where was my own blood? I desire it to mingle here with His, for on this Cross I wish to die. There is nothing left for me, Mother, for I "gave myself away," as my missionary so beautifully put it. Yes, I should be in my new home soon, and so I shall return Father's lovely relic, and I desire to be even more there for him. The nights I've kissed and embraced this sacred relic, when its imprint was left upon my heart, I desired to be left upon its form also. And I am weeping, sobbing to think of how I've fought the nails that Christ has deigned to take from His Hands to place in mine, so that I might stay there until I have breathed my soul to God. But here are my hands, my twisted feet. Take them to Him NOW, Mother. Take them before I have a chance to draw back in fear. And you, my beautiful Mother, hold them to that sacred wood until every limb has been fastened to that sacred wood and I have been left there to die. And then, Mother, when all is consummated and there is nothing left for me but my miserable poverty, take my limp form in your arms, wash it in your tears, wrap it in your immaculate garments, and offer it to God. How might He refuse anything from you? And how might He receive anything without you? Mary, my Queen, my Mother, I am yours!

two

～ِع9ْ～

SEPTEMBER 5, 1962, TO DECEMBER 23, 1962

---

irginia recounts her struggles as she leaves the one and only home she has ever known and moves into Good Samaritan Nursing Home in Kokomo, Indiana, usually referred to as "Sam." This will be her home base for the remainder of her short life. She takes a trip to Gary, Indiana, to visit Sister Blanche, someone with whom she had corresponded for years but until then had never met. In Kokomo she begins to make new friends, chief among them Jean Black. With the approval and encouragement of its members, Virginia works to transform a church "coffee club" into a Jesus-Caritas-type fraternity. Her prayer is to be nothing but an instrument of God's grace. She writes: "Spirit of Love, here are my lips and my heart. Use them for Love, only Love. Use them as You use those of my missionary, for my missionary, so that like him I may pour Christ into every soul. O Soul of my soul, annihilate me in Love."

A. J. P. M.
[*Ad Jesum per Mariam* — "To Jesus through Mary"]

Wednesday, September 5, 1962
[Virginia visits her future home]

Mother dear, what a way to begin my second book of letters to you. I just gave the first to Father Keith today. As you well know, I just couldn't bear to give these letters to anyone else, but I do want my missionary to share in all that I do for him, just as I am now able to be his partner in spreading the love of Christ in the Gospel to all "our" people. I thank God each second for permitting this union between us, and then I offer the joy of that second for Father Keith. Please take this tiny "Charlie" heart, so full and yet so frail, and fill it with your joyful *Magnificat* till it can overflow before the throne of God. May God Almighty smile and bless my missionary through the tears of his little sister.

Mother, it's hard to realize that this is the first time in thirteen years that I am not getting ready to go back to school. Yes, even the past two years I returned to SJA with the students. But now God has asked me to continue my education elsewhere. Never will I cease to learn. And now I shall be my class. And today I met my new teachers; trained in the excellent school of suffering for many hard years, till finally they were sent to teach me. And so, as I begin once again, I beg the Holy Spirit to teach this little one to speak — and understand. Mother, please help me with my homework.

There was such a note of finality in this visit to Good Samaritan, and I felt that in that moment when we drove up to the open door of my new home, I bid farewell to Elwood, but all the "Charlies" moved into that hospital with me. And I was happy.

Sister Raphael showed me around the building. My room is a very small quarter right by the elevator on the first floor. I was trying so hard to see everything that I can hardly remember what it's like. I do know that it's quite small and I'll have to go through my belongings and eliminate quite a few things. But that's good, for they really pile up over the years. And now I have an excellent chance to exercise my vow of poverty, and I beg the strength to do it as God wills. Only a little room, nothing pretty, one small locker and a dresser, an elevator that I can't operate alone but must ask help each time I wish to use it; the cheery little chapel all the way on second floor with access only if someone takes me; alone except for the priest whose room adjoins mine, and yet I feel that this is a very wonderful thing for me.

O POVERTY, can it be that at last I have found a little part of your countenance? If so, I thank God that He has permitted me to follow Brother Charles here to live with and bring Christ into the home of these elderly people. I beg the chance to go among these, my older brothers and sisters, every now and then so that I might get to know and love each of them, and spend myself in bringing love and happiness into their long and lonesome days. I've never had this privilege before and beg you to teach me to use it as I should. Sister M. Aquinas is to be my guardian angel, and I just know that I will love her. We'll have many happy times together, and I thank you for arranging everything so beautifully for God's little vagabond.

Monday, September 10

Father was so kind to permit me to go to Confession this morning. Mother, I tried so hard to talk of many things which I felt were important, but the finality of this entire week and the pain that gnaws at my heart in leaving Father and the others grew almost unbearable, and only tears spilled where words were too insufficient to say what I wished. And I know that Father understood just what I wished to say. He always does. O how I love him! And he told me to offer for each one this pain I have in leaving those I love. And he must know just how much I shall endure for him. For my penance he told me to try hard to forget the departure, to enjoy the few days I have left here. Please help me do this, for if I try it myself I find it impossible.

How I wish I might bid each of the "Charlies" farewell a day at a time! It would take that long to thank each of them for all the lessons on love they've given me this summer. And as for Velma and Leo, I lose words when I wish to thank them. Here I've found Nazareth, and it took Christ thirty years to thank you for that. But help me to somehow show them the gratitude that fills my heart. Protect "our" Holy Family, always!

Thursday, September 13

This evening after dinner, Velma and I sat together at the table, listening to lovely music. She asked me something that has never struck me before. She asked if I consider what I received this summer worth all the pain I must endure now. Never shall I doubt that the price I must now pay is microscopic in return for *Amicitia. Deo gratias*!

Saturday, September 15 (Feast of Your Tears)

Velma, Leo, and I attended Holy Mass together this morning. Thank you for permitting me to share, in my own miserable little way, your terrible sufferings. Just as those seven swords engraved Christ's I love you on your tender Mother's heart, so let these aches, which I, fool that I am, must bear for Christ; let these serve to mold your little slave to be more and more like her Mother. During today's sermon, Father Keith spoke directly to me. Even Velma noticed that. And so, in our farewell, he told me to learn to suffer as you did. That's a big order, but I can do so if you will teach me. Speak, Mother dear. Your little one awaits her lesson for today.

We were in the car and driving from my lovely Nazareth about two. I tried to look at everything so that I might never forget a detail of the spot in which I had found such peace and joy. Although my vision was blurred by the tears which came no matter how hard I tried to suppress them, still I knew that I was taking this Nazareth with me, not the beauty of its buds but its seeds, to be planted wherever God's little vagabond is sent.

The drive to Kokomo was very difficult. I tried so hard to be funny, to laugh, but is it possible to hide all that from one who knows you too well? Not really, but please accept my effort and tell her that I am very happy to be doing God's Holy Will, no matter how it hurts.

Velma and Leo stayed to help me get settled, and then came the inevitable farewell and the tears that I shed no matter how hard I tried to hold them back. But I have yet to find that corner and really let them flow freely as Father suggested. When I am with these two, then I want to do all in my power to hide my hurts from them; and when I'm with others I know that to be myself would only confuse them. O please give me your shoulder! I need you, Mother, right now, to soothe a heart that aches because it has just been torn from those it loves most. In one summer I grew to treasure everything in that lovely Nazareth. Please teach me to bring all these treasures here to those who in their kindness have volunteered to be my new family.

Sunday, September 16 [First full day at Good Sam]

We had Holy Mass at seven this morning. Sister Aquinas came in about six to see if I was up. And there I was dressing on the floor. She is so very kind to me, and I could just hug her for all the smiles and niceties she gives me. And I do hug her at times, so there!

The morning literally flew by, and before I knew anything Sister had brought my dinner. I just don't know how I'm going to put away all they bring me, but I eat all that fits, and then get a funny little look from Sister and get by with it.

Sister saw to it that I took my nap, and a very good one I had. Guess the fatigue I've been fighting for so long is showing on the outside, but what with my guardian angel caring for me, the one in the pretty white veil who notices all little telltale signs, I should feel great in no time. I do hope so, for this time it's been a month and a half since I've felt really up to par. But this time I gained a missionary during the cycle. And so I beg that I shall always have something to give for him, so that the distance which has painfully taken me further from him will bring us ever closer together in the love of Christ.

Wednesday, September 19

These weeks have been difficult for me. The pain and fatigue have been constant companions, and when the drain of settling in a new home was added, your little one had to lean hard on her Mother to survive. Thank you for always being here with me, you who understand pain and tears as no mother ever will. And now let me get strong so I can do a little work for my new family. Yes, *fiat*! It must be Christ's work, as He wishes to perform it through me. Let me never do anything of myself.

Thursday, September 20

Just as Sister brought in my supper tray, I saw Daddy drive up. So, as all spoiled little girls are wont to do, I convinced Daddy that he was dying to take me to a movie. Actually, it wasn't legitimate, for I used waterworks.

Saturday, September 22

It's a good thing I didn't see the postman today. You know me, "Charlie" that I am. What with all the goodies he brought me I probably would have given him a squeeze and a smacker.

Our dear "Charlie" at the Nazareth I long for wrote me a precious epistle. How thrilled I was to hear from her. And if you offered for me the pain that accompanied the tears which fell as I read each treasured word, then I know that you didn't forget to polish the joy also. It seems that my entire life must be one of thanksgiving, and yet if you don't help me I can never begin to express my gratitude to Our Father. Mother, do teach me your *Magnificat*, so that we can sing together.

Velma states that she thinks it was a mistake to try to make me a member of the family. She says it's just too cruel when it can't be permanent. And she begged forgiveness for the pain I've suffered! O Mother, do tell her that I'd return only to leave a thousand Nazareths, if only I might learn each time a little better the lessons of LOVE I found there. Ah yes, the chisel hurts as it pulls me from the only "home" there ever was, but it must keep hurting till the Sculptor has His little heap of humanity as He wishes. Hold me tight right here in your hands, and then tell Him to whittle where He wishes till He has formed a suitable plaything.

Monday, October 1

Weakness and joy, this was what today brought my missionary. And when I was handed a bookmark right before my holy hour this afternoon that read MAY THE HEART OF JESUS BE EVERYWHERE LOVED, my poor little heart danced in its glee. And I begged that hour would never end, so tightly did I feel entwined in the arms of my Beloved. All day this experience has given me even physical strength. True, I couldn't pull myself from the chair, but I felt that no feat would be too much for me. Christ's strength. And His Cross. These are the possessions that I pray will never be taken from me. Now let this happy child sleep in your arms, smiling in a dream that was TODAY.

Wednesday, October 3 (Feast of St. Thérèse of Lisieux)

Mother, little Thérèse hurled lovely little rose petals constantly today, and each one that came my way — and they were many — I blew softly so that it might fall upon my missionary and bring to him the joy it brought his littlest sister. Filled with pain and weakness, little sister pain took "this earthly clod and flung it up to God." Please kiss each little petal so that one day I might be God's little flower, and I shall become a rose of suffering for my missionary sprinkled with the dew of his blessings.

Sunday, October 7

Please hug me close. I've felt so lonely today. How foolish your little one is. She who received Christ this morning knows loneliness? Beg Him to forgive me and show me again and again how to love Him. My patient Mother, I shall try again and again to learn. O to live one day that I might not hurt my Spouse!

Monday, October 8

Father Keith wrote me during "our" retreat. Thank you, my precious Mother, for permitting this treasure to your little weakling. Each word fell as a soft shower on my lonely heart, and then I found my fountain being filled and I spilled all this love to God. And it was good to cry as I knelt there before your picture and knew that you offered so many little gems for my missionary. Thank you for always being here, always loving me and understanding me when there is no other shoulder I might cry on.

Remember when I used to pray that my poor Mama might return and stay with us "forever and ever, till the end of the world"? In return I have a Mother who will be mine for eternity. What shall I return to the Lord for all He has given me? I will take the chalice of salvation. Hold it to my lips, Mother. My hands are not steady, but with your assistance I drink. And may that which is bitter to my tongue become the height of refreshment to my heart. The cure IS what's killing me. Hasten the day when my soul will love nothing of this world, when it will be dead to the world in the life of the Father, Son, and Holy Spirit.

Wednesday, October 10

O Mother, I fear that I am too tired to tell Him what I should, but do embrace Christ for me. Tell Him that I wish I might return the tiniest fraction of the Love He showered upon His little wretch today. This is utterly impossible, unless I love Him with your Immaculate Heart. I am your littlest slave, the clumsiest of those who serve you, one whose little capers you tolerate, and you even take me into your arms and kiss me for my clumsiness. Take me now, and as I snuggle here, sing my *Magnificat* to God. And I know that He will smile, and I shall sleep here and be refreshed by your kiss.

Thursday, October 11 (Feast of Your Motherhood)

Happy Feast day, Mother! You whose *fiat* was so strong that what was uttered by a hidden maiden to an angel in Nazareth echoed through space and time to the mouth of a Mother standing on a hill, whose tear-stained eyes gazed at the lifeless Body of her Son. In that one *fiat* you exchanged your eternal Son for a little wretch just beginning her climb. Why, Mother? Although I shall never understand, I shall be eternally grateful. I shall keep struggling. With you there to beckon me I know that one day I, too, shall reach the top, there to fling myself upon His Holy Cross. Mother, keep calling me. Show me the blood-stained path. And if I fall, weak as I am, draw me in your strong motherly caress.

Mrs. Black and Mrs. Read came this morning with the prescription Father Keith had asked them to get filled for me. They are so very enthusiastic about Father's suggestion that I help them impregnate their coffee club with "Charlie." They were thrilled when I gave them the JESUS+CARITAS booklet on

"Friendship" and another on the life of Brother Charles. I do get the Willies when I think of the silly little instrument the Holy Spirit plans to use for this, but then I remind myself that my part is only to be His plaything, completely abandoned to His good pleasure. Please watch me, Mother, that I never drift from His sight.

Saturday, October 13

Sister let me go to Mrs. Ryan's room this morning for our first instruction. I think she'll do fine, God love her. This is a completely new experience for me, and once more I drew upon my missionary's unlimited Source, the Holy Spirit. Would that I might be such a supple instrument as He! Teach me, sweet spouse of the Holy Spirit. Let me be so filled with Love that, like him, I may be another Christ. Love of Christ, my true identity, consume me completely in your Flames. Only then might I be a worthy co-missionary. What movement of divine grace moved me to pledge myself to this Cross as Father's little Simon? A mere infant who asks to shoulder a giant's burden? LOVE does such things! That's all. I know that only you can really understand. Thank you, my Mother.

Monday, October 15 (Feast of St. Teresa of Ávila)

At adoration this afternoon Christ kissed me so gently. And I tried to find Him. There He was in the tabernacle. Here He was within me. But no, this was a different presence. He was everywhere. I couldn't move from His embrace. I was in Him. Please, Jesus, let me stay!

Saturday, October 20

Mother, why does it hurt so? Will I ever be free of this nagging pain? I'm so very tired. My body begs to lie on a comfy bed and truly rest. Yes, the flesh is truly weak, for I know that deep down pervades a great joy in suffering. I guess each time I go to the clinic I expect something of a cure, but when it doesn't happen and I see that I may keep this for my missionary, you know how I rejoice. Thank you for telling me just how I might share in his apostolate of Love. And yes, I'll keep this misery as long as you'll permit. With Love, take this to him, my precious brother.

Saturday, October 27

Had planned to have the daily catechism lesson with Mrs. Ryan after my bath this morning, but I just couldn't push any further. Mother, I try with all my feeble ability to hide this pain, never to utter a complaint, to smile Christ's smile to all I meet. But still there are some who see through my front. And when I asked to go to my room without having started the lesson, everyone knew something was wrong. Do forgive me, and help me to work much harder for my missionary. Every day I shall begin again the lessons Father teaches us with his life, the life of Christ. Please help me, Mother.

Sunday, October 28 (Feast of Christ the King)

Your little one wished to run before her King today, throwing flowers in His path. But instead she sat here, waiting for His shadow to bathe her, then only to smile and to know that He understood the little smile upon my lips that screamed the love of you in my heart. And in chapel this evening, my heart wept because I hadn't the strength to make His Way of the Cross with Him or even to say any of my night prayers except your Little Crown. I only sat there, happy to be with Him and knowing that He accepted my poverty, all that was mine to give today for my little brother. *Deo gratias!*

Jean Black returned with the "Friendship" booklet and the wonderful news that this Thursday evening we'll have our first get-together with the coffee club that desires to grow up, to become "Charlies." I feel completely incapable of helping them, and I AM. But the Holy Spirit can and will do all things He wishes with His silly little instrument. God is my Father, and you my Mother. So I have no reason for NOT being a cock-eyed optimist. And I AM.

Monday, October 29

What in the world was my missionary up to last night? Whatever it was, I'm sure he loved much. He always does. Meanwhile, back at Good Sam, I had quite the night. How very uncomfortable every position has become. I went from the floor to the chair, until exhaustion finally took over from midnight till 3:45.

Mother, I want to write more to you, to tell you once again how I love you, to thank you a thousand times for taking this misery for my dear missionary. But I know that you understand all this, so I must go to rest. Please let it be always more, for if you, my precious Mother, stay with me always, then and only then can I give Father all I must, all you've asked me to give him. I can write no longer. My head is spinning and I can hardly read what I'm writing you now. O this joy! If I were strong enough I would sing a beautiful love song. But my heart is singing. *Deo gratias!*

Wednesday, October 31

Mother Madeleine wrote from Our Lady of Hope. I was happy to hear from our dear Sisters. Please let me see them soon, that is, if you think it best for me. Actually, I needn't ask for anything, Mother, for you are always showering me with your loving care. And yet, like a little child, once in a while I come for a piece of candy. And because I am so young and ignorant of those things I really need, you bend to give it to me with a kiss. You don't get the same romping and thank-you kisses when you give me my vitamins, do you, Mother? But I shall try to learn that anything you give me is good, and I want to thank you for yucky medicine, too, even if I do make a horrible face in doing so.

Thursday, November 1 (All Saints' Day)

Thank you, dear Queen of all saints, for making our day such a lovely one. Please give my love to all our dear friends there with you, to Joseph, Anthony, Bernadette, Thérèse; also to some little Virginia who lived on wheels and rolled steadily closer to God. Is she there now, to be just a little blossom at her Mother's feet? Do ask her to let me join her one of these days.

I love you, Mother. How can so very many of your children forget you? I shall tell them, Mother. I'll show them just how you've cared for me. And perhaps you are laughing at this zeal. It is rather foolish of one so very insignificant to aspire to be your campaign manager, but when I hear the words "It is no longer I..." whispering within me, I know that I can do all things.

This evening we held our first "Charlie" meeting in Kokomo. O the dynamic response of those eight! Thank you, Mother, a thousand thank you's, for sending the Spirit of Christ to work so beautifully in our midst. We spoke of friendship and I formed friendships, eternal I pray. But now it's so very late. Please forgive me for having kept Sister, and you, up so late, and teach me the prudence and consideration that Christ wishes to have through me in all things.

Sunday, November 4

After Holy Mass this morning, our precious Jesus was exposed for our Holy Thirteen Hours here at Good Samaritan. Please tell Him how we wish to thank Him for such great condescension. And tell Him how very sorry I am that I could not be a better companion for Him as I stayed with Him today. I yearned to love Him, to be there with Him and with nothing to come between us, but the pains were so severe. My neck, arms, back, legs — there was nowhere I didn't feel its scourge. Finally I found the muscle spasms just too exhausting, so I climbed to the floor, there to kneel in painful expression of my love. I know He accepted this poor love, for You gave it to Him for me. Please thank Him that He permitted me to love Him thus. For He knows that, did He not give me this wonderful suffering, I would have nothing to offer.

Sunday, November 11

O Mother, when you plan delights for your little one you really go all the way, don't you? We had a truly beautiful weekend! It's impossible to thank you properly, but I know that you accept my silly efforts.

Daddy came right after my holy hour Thursday, very much earlier than I had anticipated. So I did a rush packing job, only to wait a half-hour while he finished a magazine article he had begun in the meantime. Then we were on our way to Gary. I must admit I was rather dreading the trip; it's always so very difficult. But then there was Sister Blanche, waiting.

Finally the moment came when we, who had known each other from thirteen years' correspondence, were introduced. And how superfluous was that introduction, for we knew each other so very well. Our beloved Sister Blanche, such an angel is she. I hugged her as an old and familiar friend, for that is precisely what she was to me. The two hours in which our visit was to have terminated proved only an appetizer. We begged Daddy to stay all night, and he gave in. Good old Dad! And so our anticipated two hours extended to two days. Thank you, dear Mother, for such prodigality for your little ones.

We had so very many happy times together, just two little children playing in Our Father's world. Guess two years wouldn't have been long enough to make up for lost time, but I feel that you gave us just the time we needed together. But then,

I'm not at all surprised, for you always do things that way for your children. Thank you, our precious Mother, thank you so very much.

Didn't know I could be so very anxious to get home. It was a long and painful ride, and I could hardly wait to see Sister Aquinas' pretty smile. After giving the gifts out, I was most anxious to rest. And our chair felt so good. And so I sat there, offering my heart once again for my missionary, filled to the brim with love and happiness, and in the shadow of the Cross, a brand new splinter this evening, that I shall lose my lovely corner here. Strip me of all but love. There must be nothing left of me, only the Love of God reigning completely through me.

Monday, November 12

Somehow losing my little corner doesn't seem so very drastic tonight. True, I shall keep this room for a study and move my clothes, etc., to the third floor for sleeping. Not that I needed more room. If there were a smaller corner available I would beg for it. The only inconvenience will be having my things so very far apart; some in a room on third and the rest down here on first, between which is the elevator that I myself am not able to manage. It will be like having to go out to work, again a Little Sister. It seems that you wish to lead me closer and closer to the ideal our dear Brother Charles has laid for us. Lead me on, blind though I am and halting though my steps. This is LOVE, thank God, and I beg for an immeasurable increase of love, YOUR love, with each breath.

Tuesday, November 13

Today Betty made trip after trip on the elevator from here to the room on third with me and all my things. There was so very much. How I wish that I had nothing to call mine, but perhaps mine is to be the poverty of possessing so very much of what I do not wish to have.

Mother, it's so very hard to keep moving like this. You know how very wearying was the move here to my new home from my beloved Nazareth. Now, only two months later, I'm obliged to have more than half my things upstairs. It's so very hard, for I cannot use the elevator alone and that's the only connection I have. No, Mother, I'm not whining. Thank God that He considers me strong enough for this. All day long, difficult though it was, I whispered, sometimes ground out, little acts of thanksgiving. To think that He considers me worthy of such vexations! His strength. Yes, I can do all things in Love.

Wednesday, November 14

Last night I felt your motherly caress as I waited for the rest that tarried in coming. Sister had fixed a chair for me in my new room, and it was fine. But I just had to get out on my knees. I've come once again to the time when sleep becomes so very precious, so rare. And I sit there awaiting it, clinging to this sacred Cross and begging that the hours I watch with Him will somehow soothe His loneliness in the tabernacle below.

Last night, as I lay there in your arms, I knew that you were trying to whisper many things to me, particularly concerning these anxieties. Yes, Mother, I must rid myself of almost all these possessions, good, precious though they be, so that I may better perform all assignments Our Father will send His littlest bum. I know that this won't be easy, but perhaps I can use these for this year's Christmas gifts. For instance, there is my First Communion dress, the plaque Joe Reilly brought us from Lourdes, the big lollipop from my missionary. Mother, these must be surrendered. Please help me to tear all these and much more from my knapsack that I may run ever so swiftly to my Jesus!

Thursday, November 15

It seems that the longer I'm away from our Nazareth the lonelier I become. No, the pain does not dull with time, as I had expected. I, with "Charlie," long for Nazareth. And instead of writing Velma this morning, as I had intended, I called. I learned that our St. Joseph will be here for me next Wednesday. Just think, Mother! Only six days from now. The fears I had as regards my going back have vanished, and now I know that you'll let me be one of them for those few days. And then I shall return alone, and be grateful for this family you loaned me. Thank you for showing me this, for showing me that love is NOW.

Saturday, November 17

We really hit the jackpot with the mailman today. Four letters! I do love this correspondence, feel that it's an integral part of my vocation, and I beg the strength to do justice to all these brothers and sisters who shower so much love upon me, who ask questions, who request prayers.

And now, Mother, please go to tell my missionary of my love for him. As he "balances his books" tonight let him find nothing that is not LOVE. And let me have nothing but LOVE to give.

Sunday, November 18

A lovely day did Jesus and I spend together. In His infinite mercy He stooped once again to enter this heart that is no longer mine. Did He find you there and smile because He was at home? Please, Mother, always be here to welcome Him. Be a Nazareth to him within me.

We wrote letters, We chatted with the girls in the kitchen, We read, We prayed, We listened to lovely music, even made some Ourselves, or We just sat here together, resting in the embrace of Love. It seemed that the angels had hushed all around Us, so as to give Us this very special day together. And now, Mother, you to whom I've been totally consecrated, you who have given me to another, take this peace to him tonight, and do tell him of my Love.

Mother, please take these tears of complete joy and of intense pain. Two months of waiting had brought me back to Nazareth. How beautiful it was. It seemed that each second was an eternity till that one in which I was wheeled into the living room to embrace Velma. And there all walls I've built while here at my new home were shattered, and I who had suppressed a thousand tears became only a poor little child crying to One Who understood. O blessed relief!

We shared a Thanksgiving meal together, I and that family I so love. How I long to say "my family," but it isn't mine. I wished to call it that but couldn't, so all weekend I tried to tell myself that I must accept this. How I wish I might learn to leave everything, family life and even earthly loves to find eternal Love. Then would I never weep again. But now I see how very distant I am from this and I shudder, until I hear your whisper reminding me that you are here and you know the way and I am your child. O to learn to fly to death and to Life.

It seemed that every second in our dear Nazareth was so precious that I wished to cling to it. How very possessive I am. Please teach me that there is only one thing to cling to, the only thing Jesus found worth taking to death. His Cross is mine. That's all, for that's Love.

Friday morning Father was so kind to hear my Confession. I may renew my vows on the Feast of your Immaculate Conception. Father thinks three times a year is good. After all, I'm usually in a different place each time. He says if I continue at this pace I might become God's little hobo. We'll keep working on it. He also suggested an appointment at the clinic before Christmas to see if anything can be done for this poor old neck of mine. But I feel that we should let it ride for a while. It seems that I run down there each time expecting a miracle, and then when I return with the same pains I wonder what happened. I must stop running from the Cross and learn to embrace it. Please help me, Mother. You know the Way.

Wednesday, November 28

Jean was here this afternoon. How happy I am when she comes, for I feel so very close to her, more so than anyone here in Kokomo. Thank you for sending me this friend in my bitter loneliness. And yet I do tremble to think that she, and the others of the group, come here looking for the spiritual advice they're so hungry to hear. Mother, I am so young, so little, only a child, and am I to speak to them the words Love wishes to utter? O Love

Jean Black and Virginia

of Christ, consume me. Let me be one with You, so that anything that is me may be annihilated in Your Flame. Let me be You incarnate!

Thursday, November 29

Please teach me to give Jesus the love you gave Him when He lived with you in quiet Nazareth. O let Him be my All. May I have no thought that is not He. I'm a fanatic? But so was He, thank God! May the world know I'm just head over heels in Love. Yes, they will treat me as they treated Him. They will ridicule and torture. And please God that they take my Jesus from that terrible tree and put me there.

Saturday, December 1

Praised be God for this day, forty-six years ago, when He brought to Little Brother Charles of Jesus the martyrdom for which he had lived each day. How my happy heart sang upon arising this morning to celebrate such a glorious day, one with all the Little Brothers and Sisters and all those of this big, gloriously happy family throughout the world to whom his legacy has been imparted.

Now it's 7:15 in the evening. There I see him kneeling in the sands of Tamanrasset. And what was going through his mind; he who had once written, "All my plans turn out to be mere bits of paper"? Did he have any conception of just how precious those papers would be to his followers? Did he see his followers? But I prefer to think that he saw none of this. I think that his most glorious report to his Lord and Brother Jesus was, "I tried." And I know Jesus smiled, maybe laughed aloud, as He embraced him and invited him to Success. For Jesus knew. He, too, had tried.

Sunday, December 2

I'm trying so hard to eliminate all the sentimental little things I've collected over the years. Only today did I discard a scrapbook. Thank God that He's finally showing me the folly of such things. Only recently has this happy freedom possessed me. Is it that at last I'm learning Holy Poverty? Remember when I renewed my vows August 15th? Poverty was the most important one then, the one in which I needed the most help. And during retreat you kindly gave me those things which might help me with this lesson. But only now am I beginning to grasp it. Here it is almost time for a renewal of those vows. Thank God that He has at last given me the graces necessary to accomplish this. The words my missionary spoke on the subject during those holy days of our retreat and the example he has since shown me were no small push for God's little vagabond. Thank you, Mother, for this big brother.

Monday, December 3

Last night I went upstairs head over heels. Remember that little saying about the harder you fall the higher you bounce? That's certainly true in Love. O the freedom that has possessed me. I think Our Father must be preparing me for something special. And now I'm all His, at last. You know, Mother, in only a few days I shall renew my vows. And I have a feeling there may be surprises in store. Remember what you pulled on me last time? How eternally grateful I am that you truly made me a little sister, just as Jesus must have planned all along. And to think that you gave me such a lover for my big brother! Remember how I begged the grace to see and accomplish God's Holy Will at Lourdes? AND that P.S. I'd love to be a Sister. Now I know that the entire prayer was answered, and not just answered but just as I had asked. Wow, it's fun to be so spoiled.

Friday, December 7

Here it is almost your Feast day again. And this Feast above all others, the Feast of your Immaculate Conception. Yes Mother, I am looking back a whole year. And I see myself on my way to the clinic with Father Keith, and I feel my heart ache because I had yearned for years to be a Bride of Christ. And then the proposal. Father is speaking to me for Christ to tell me I may be entirely His, I may bind myself in Poverty, Chastity and Obedience. And then the stop at the bookstore and in my hands was a little gray book that was to change my life. There was a heart in red, surmounted by a Cross, and the book *Seeds In The Desert*. And then permission to make private temporary vows on December 8th. And now, one year later, it is only a matter of hours till I run to Christ again and lay my nothing-ness at His feet and receive in return His Love.

Saturday, December 8 (Your Immaculate Conception)

Who am I that the Mother of my Lord should come to me? With Elizabeth I listen to your response to her question, her awe. And within my heart echoes the song that sprang to your lips. Our Mother, wrapped in the silence of one in God's Presence, suddenly breaks into song among those she knew and loved. Ah yes, Mother, I understand, for I, too, have felt this freedom, and have sung. And if there was nothing in this little heart of mine today but Love's freedom song, I know you let it blend with yours.

Monday, December 10

Did Baby Jesus laugh at me this afternoon as I spent my hour before Him, so very anxious to know that He will accept the little stable you and I are preparing for Him this Advent that I just couldn't stifle the songs we save for His Birthday? I bet He thought our record got stuck, for I could think of noth-ing but the little drummer boy and his gift. And though I wished to sing to Jesus about it, for I find it silly to hide these things from Him, I didn't know all the words and had fun ad-libbing. Please tell Him thank you for tolerating me there, let-ting me stay at His feet for an hour each day, with nothing to do but listen for His voice, whisper little love secrets, just to be there. Please tell Him I appreciate this bit of heaven, this bit of Home for which even vagabonds yearn.

Tuesday, December 11

Today I received the long-prayed-for news that on Christmas day the missionary you've given me will join the Jesus-Caritas Sacerdotal Union. How very thrilled I am at this, for it seems just one more bond that binds my life to Jesus-Caritas. For you've given my life to him. And now our life is to be spent in Jesus-Caritas. This pattern becomes more and more clearly evident to me. I come closer each day to Nazareth, and somehow I know now that you've kept me from convents, etc., plagued me with confusion and disappointments, so that at last I might find this very special path hewn from eternity for God's Little Vagabond. Yes, like Brother Charles, blindly shall I live and die, my feeble attempts and failures swallowed in another's success, our success, a missionary and his shadow.

Sunday, December 23

This morning the Holy Gospel shouted at us to make ready, Jesus is coming. Yes, Jesus, come. There is room for You. You see, your Mother and I have worked all during Advent to prepare this little spot for You to cuddle in. None other will fill it but You, King of Kings. And there is nothing minute enough to fit here but the majestic Simplicity of You, glorious Baby. *Veni, veni, Emmanuel!*

When Daddy and I returned to Sam today, what should delight our eyes but the lovely array of birthday presents left for me to open for the Baby? O Mother, it was so fantastic. Every corner glittered. There were big and small surprises, cards, letters, prayer stipends. It was a breathtaking spectacle. Chair, record player, fireplace, tree, table, everything smiled a joyous Birthday smile. Yes, Mother, thank you for letting me be here to receive all this

Virginia, circa 1963

from Him. And in receiving I must return to all these souls His Love. Come, Lord Jesus. We shall love them together; rather YOU shall love them through me. Jesus-Caritas! O Mother, fill the entire world with it. Let everything glow in its flames. And together we shall light the world. Baby Jesus, Mother and a very little sister. *Fiat*! And the Word lives in my very flesh.

three

DECEMBER 30, 1962, TO JUNE 19, 1963

---

*V*irginia continues working to transform a church coffee club into a prayer group based upon Jesus–Caritas principles. Key participants in the group are Jean Black, Mary Romack, and Lou Deschamps. She takes another trip to Gary, Indiana, to visit Sister Blanche. Her contact with her many friends from Elwood, Indiana, continues, despite the distance that separates them. She petitions to become an official member of the Jesus–Caritas lay fraternity, but is refused admission. This leads her friend, Father Lucien Duesing, to write the insightful words, "You have so many and varied interests that I feel that you can never belong to anybody or any one organization because you must belong to everybody. You are without a home to be 'at home' everywhere." Virginia feels a growing desire to attain a spirituality rooted in silence, one that emphasizes the virtues of womanhood and the motherhood of Mary. She comes to understand better and accept the unique vocation she has been given. She writes, "I feel so convinced of my work, so sure that it's what Our Father wants, because I've had no part in planning it so." She also makes her first visit to St. Meinrad Archabbey in Southern Indiana.

A. J. P. M.
[*Ad Jesum per Mariam* — "To Jesus through Mary"]

Sunday, December 30, 1962

Here I am today, Mother, in the little corner you've readied for me. How long will you keep me here? Our Father decides such things. It is for you, my precious Mother, to whisper His wishes to me, and in His strength I shall do all things Love requests. Aunt Vivian is trying to bring some definite plans into my vagabond life again. She wishes to help, I know, but I just can't explain to her what I truly feel is my vocation. She doesn't think I belong here and wishes to relocate me. Mother, I do feel that you've brought me here for a purpose. So it is very hard for me. But I can't run from Love's demands. No Mother, I shall remain to finish the work you've assigned here, then skip to the next task on eternity's path.

Monday, December 31

Now it is nearing the end of the year of our beloved Lord and Brother Jesus, 1962. What must be my resolution? When I asked Father Keith this question, his answer was simple and clear: "Poverty." Yes, Mother, the Baby King has spoken. There He lies on His bed of straw, soon to lie upon the rough wood of a tree. And He asks me to stay there with Him. O where else is there to go? Must He ask me? Mother, please lay me there, wrapped in Love, annihilated in its Flames. And when you look down into that poor manger, may you see only your Baby, Jesus!

Tuesday, January 1
(In the Year of Our Beloved Lord
and Brother Jesus, 1963)

Mary Romack was here all afternoon. Thank you for sending her. We spoke very intimately of the things of God. It is at times like these, when troubled souls spill out their pains, that I know Jesus is truly present. And I never fear that what I say might be the wrong thing. With His Love within me I know I can do no harm. And without this Love may I never utter a sound. Happiness — the hunger to give. O Mother, I am so very happy in Christ.

Wednesday, January 2

I was so very surprised to receive a lovely message from Sister M. Peter, who taught me in the third and fourth grade at St. Vincent's Villa. Thank you, Mother, for this note of encouragement. To think of the love in which you've surrounded me all my life overwhelms me. Through tears and laughter alike you were here with me, caressing your little child. May this prodigality always fall on a child pleasing to our loving Father.

Sunday, January 6 (Little Christmas)

Need a little advice, Mother. It seems that lately my desire to join JCF [*Jesus-Caritas Fraternity*] is increasing continually and abundantly. Is this simply that I love "Charlie" so or an indication of Our Father's Will in this matter? Please ask Him for me. Perhaps I can talk it over with Anne-Marie. One thing I fear is that my vagabond life might not be compatible with the rule. And I do feel He wishes this way for me. *Fiat*. I'll await His call. Only use me for His glory, Mother. That's all.

Wednesday, January 9

This morning I wrote a note to Father Keith, telling him of this burning desire to join JCF and asking his advice. Whatever he says will be my will, for I know he will use Christ's words for me. Be Our Mother always. We both love you.

Thursday, January 10

We had a great meeting at Pat's this morning. Mother, I see the many little miracles of grace with which the Holy Spirit is encouraging us and I rejoice to know that it is His Will we perform. With each meeting we sound depths in communication so new to this group. Live, Jesus, in our Love!

Jean and I stopped for a Big Boy [*hamburger*] before returning home. It's very hard to express the gratitude I feel that God should permit me to love this beautiful soul. Each time we're together I feel the bond between us tighten, and each time I marvel that it is possible that our love should increase still more. This must be Heaven. Boundless Love, I run to You!

Friday, January 11

Our bumpers broke last night, and I looked so funny with a big brown belt around everything. I knew I had to keep them on somehow to get a little rest, and this morning the pain and muscle spasms were sheer agony. Thank you, Mother; I just know you took each pang immediately for my missionary. And with such a consolation I could be nothing but filled with joy. Guess the girls on third wondered that I could be chattering away happily one minute and the next be wrenched with pain. O but this is Love. And Christ has no back, no neck or arms or legs or head but mine in which to continue His Passion of Love. Could I bear to refuse this request? Live, Jesus! And besides, how could I have known just how much God spares me with this luxury unless I felt its relief this afternoon after a whole morning without it? Thank God for bumpers!

Sister Aquinas "warned" me today concerning my love for Jean. I had mentioned something about Jean, and Sister kindly gave me a lesson on the dangers of personal friendships. Although it rather amused me, it didn't create a striking conversion. Sometimes I could burst with the joy these "dangerous" friendships you've permitted me bring. I sorta like living dangerously if this is it. I think Jesus lived the same way. Love does such things!

Saturday, January 12

Dear Mother, I fear exhaustion and pain are to be constant companions for a while. Today told me what before I refused to hear. I'm so tired, Mother. As the day wore on, the pain increased, and this evening it is truly my dear companion, kissing me every-where, all over my back, neck, arms, and legs. Please help me to hide it better this time than I have before. Then no one need know what special little goodies Jesus sends, and in Him I can do all things. How else might I begin to love You? I can't begin, but I can only let Your Spirit possess me. Then You shall live in me and I can LOVE.

[*For the first time (page 19, volume three), Virginia began a page of her "Letters" with the word "LOVE" with a cross (+) above it. Until now, every page had begun with the abbreviation "A.J.P.M." The next two pages reverted back to the letters "A.J.P.M.," but after that she used nothing but the new symbol, or a hand-drawn heart surmounted by a cross.*]

+

LOVE

Monday, January 14

It's such fun to sit here and look back upon all my shattered dreams, only to find that they were not magnificent enough to fit the Eternal Thought of God. And so they were shattered to build these eternal structures.

Father Keith sent a message, "Okay." O thank you, Mother. Now I know Christ wants me in Jesus-Caritas, and I just can't wait to speak with Anne-Marie. What will she say to her "*petite soeur?*" Perhaps in her kindness she will permit me into her family in spite of my childishness. Perhaps she will smile at the capers of the little sparrow like you do, Mother.

Sunday, February 3

Your little one is quite incapable, physically and spiritually, of expressing the gratitude that surges in my poor little heart for all that you have done for me since I last wrote. But you understand, don't you, Mother? And yet you encourage me to continue these little love notes to you. You who know each second of a life entirely dedicated to Christ through your sweet maternal hands, you must smile upon my futile attempts to write to you of events born in God's eternal Word. And you love me so, me with such weaknesses and failures, that you encourage me to continue to write you because through these letters you may teach me the Way and the Truth and the Life.

Daddy did come for me Friday, January 18th, to take me for a weekend with our darling Sister Blanche. But YOU had even bigger plans for us, didn't you, Mother? And when your little one so anticipated that little time with Sister, you saw fit to give me THREE weekends, over two weeks, at the big hospital where Jesus seems to speak so very clearly. Thank you for the retreat there. I know not why you chose Gary, Indiana, to bring me such refreshment. But I need know nothing but that I have a Mother who loves me eternally. And I snuggle in your arms. No wonder it's so easy to smile.

In Gary I found a doctor who has won my confidence, Dr. Jahns. He kindly agreed to help a vagabond, after Sister Blanche had explained my problems. Doc thinks I'm both spastic and athetoid. See, always spoiled, including TWO types of cerebral palsy. Upon seeing me he immediately ordered a collar for this poor neck of mine; a felt cervical collar so that the muscle spasms would find a little give in the brace. You, Mother, who know my little plans, you know how I've wished for something like this to bring me relief. Of course, I knew I needn't tell you about it. How could a very little one explain to her Mother what is needed? Only to sit here and love you. That's why Jesus lets me sit with Him at your feet, lie here in your arms, completely confident that every need will be fulfilled.

Doc told me to abandon the crutches. What with my lack of balance I used to fall so very often. And he says that if I should break a bone I'd be in a real pickle, for it could never heal with all my muscle spasms. I wanted only to know what I ought to do. And now, instead of tripping at your heels as you take me to Jesus, I nestle in your arms as you carry me to my Spouse.

Wednesday morning, braced from head to toe for just about anything, we met Dr. Jahns in the cast room, and he followed us to my room with a harness and five pounds of traction. Then he demonstrated for us. It looked so easy and sounded so wonderful that I might be in bed again. I kicked for joy, and after he left, Sister and I both dripped [*tears*] for joy. Then I started making plans to call several friends FROM BED. It all sounded like a dream. Remember how I've always said I'll dive for that first cloud beyond the Golden Gates? Well, I was going to tell everyone I was calling from heaven.

O Mother, it was terrifying. I lay there stretched out flat in traction for two eternal minutes, every muscle in my aching body twitching in violent spasms. And when the others could stand to see me lie there no longer, only two minutes of my Jesus' three hours on His bed of agony, I was pulled to a sitting position, there to sit shaking, sobbing, mingling my feeble tears with those of Love dropped from Sister's eyes. Why the tears in my eyes? Did I really wish to lie down that much? No, Mother, that is so unimportant to me. I guess I had seen in my mind's eye the happiness on the faces of each of my friends as I told them to make the bed for me. It's not hard to accept the judgments of others anymore, of those who think that my sleeping position indicates a mental condition or who are constantly telling me that I needn't be so ascetical. But to be so close to all these Christ has given me that they are hurt by my pain and insomnia. Maybe this is just a little shadow of dear Jesus' tears as He saw you beneath His Cross. And Love does such things! *Accipio.*

Sister put me in traction again for an hour the next afternoon, then Sunday evening prayed over her decision to drop the whole business. I didn't know whether to hug her or argue that I must keep trying. But I hugged her. It was a blessed relief to know that I might rest a little that night. My entire body had been twisting violently in spasms all day Saturday and Sunday. The pain was terrific, and wonderful. O thank you, Mother! In my recent letters to you, I begged that you'd help me do my share in my missionary's apostolate. I embrace the parcel you've sent that I might give. Please tell my little brother somehow that I love him and I'm so happy to be the least of his flock.

It was so very difficult to bid goodbye to all the wonderful friends Christ gave me there at the hospital of our Mother's mercy, and I couldn't bear to think of saying farewell to Sister. I was too choked up for words. We who remain together in THE Word need say nothing. Christ has said it all as He spreads His arms to embrace the world, pressing each of us to His Sacred Heart.

Thursday, February 14

Today it is customary to send to those we love greetings to tell them so. So recently I've strewn all the contents of my knapsack, trying to find therein a gift worthy of my beautiful Mother. There was only miserable poverty. And so with tear-stained cheeks I turn my face to you. Do you find it here, the one valentine that can delight you eternally? Do you see Christ and magnify your God? Do you hasten to caress in me the little Jesus you held centuries ago? Only then shall I have offered you a valentine. If you will but steady my hands, I offer Love NOW.

Sister Aquinas was here this morning, telling me how wrong it is of me to keep going as I do. If only I might make her see some things. Of course, I feel yucky at times; these spasms wear me out. But does that mean I'm to sit down and call it quits? I truly don't consider Holy Obedience's commands thus. If I don't love to the hilt TODAY, how can I assure myself of another chance? Life is too short and too exciting.

It is most important that I keep going. I thank God for every opportunity to go out among souls and bring His Presence there. I give of myself, my strength, my time, my Love, all the glorious experiences with which God has conditioned me for such a vocation. And I beg that this self I wish to be consumed in the multitudes may be none other than Christ. How else might I serve? I can't imagine another way for me, for there is no other way. Jesus asks that His life be thus in me. O the eternal tragedy of refusing! No, I can't refuse. And each obstacle will be only a stepping stone if you but hold my hand. Mother, I love you so!

Saturday, February 16

Mother, you know how Jesus loved at Nazareth, you who of all God's creatures were most like His Son. Do show me how to love those He has given me, especially those in whom His image is marred by fallen humanity. But He's there. The sanctuary light is O so dim, but it is there. Perhaps I cannot even distinguish it, but I know that only death can put it out. And there is nothing to enflame it but my love. But if I feel so distant from these, is it not that Jesus' life has not become mine completely? If He truly lives here I shall love these. If He in His infinite Wisdom loves them so in spite of their wretchedness, not because of it, who am I to turn from them, I who am one of the ugliest among them? Please ask that in His exquisite kindness He may once more knock at my door. And whereas before I might have opened it a little to converse with Him, to give Him of my time, of myself, now I wish to fling that door open as far as it will.

Wednesday, February 20

I got so very sick at our get-together this morning, but managed to appear normal till five minutes after Jean and Barbara dropped me off. You know, Mother, after I've been in such misery I always feel so good to be well again. I just know it's worth everything I give in my wretchedness when at last I get a little relief. That's like heaven, isn't it, Mother? We live these few years in exile to be eternally happy when we get Home. Our feeble minds have to grasp what a thing is NOT before we can begin to grasp the eternal reality of God. And God is LOVE. Anything we learn beyond that is useless, and yet in learning to love we've learned the ultimate Truth of life. I throw myself at your feet. Please tell me of Jesus.

Thursday, February 21

Bug's all gone, and strength too. And yet who am I to say whether I've given more today in my nothingness than I've given on those days of heavy correspondence or much visiting or long hours in chapel? Sense of value? I have none. Jesus is our Judge, and not even He until we get Home. But on the road? What does it matter? Only to be His little hobo, to be Christ today, completely abandoned to His every wish. He wishes to be a poor cripple on wheels, He wishes only to smile today, He is tired and so must rest. Live, Jesus!

Sunday, February 24

During adoration after dinner the idea of sacrifice over-whelmed me, and my little pencil burst out in song when I realized the tremendous priestly office given each of us. I, too, am permitted to say my Mass! O holy angels, hushed before such an ugly creature given such noble privileges, let me join my praise to yours.

Tuesday, February 26

You know, yesterday evening Sister Josepha came in to see if I had any candy and caught me writing to you. Then and again today I was ridiculed. But I know you don't mind my writing you. Of course, you know about "things." And yet I'm sure a Mother doesn't mind finding little love notes strewn by a child who loves Her so. There are O so many ways of saying I love you. And I'm going to use every one I find!

Tell Jesus I've written Anne-Marie at last, and now it is only a matter of her reply and I shall know if I may become an official member of the Jesus-Caritas family. Jesus knows how long I've been at home with them. And whether I may be the very least among those little sisters, or just the little tramp that gladly takes the multitude of crumbs that fall from Jesus-Caritas to the world, I shall be happy. Anywhere Jesus wants me, He knows His little hobo will be happy if He's there. I know that this is one lollipop I can always cling to.

Ash Wednesday, February 27

Today, Holy Mother Church reminded us that we are but dust. How thrilling were these words Father spoke to me as he placed that Lenten reminder upon my brow. I was thrilled by the thought that Jesus loved this little heap of mud to death, that He flung Himself joyfully upon a tree to die because He knew that I and the poorest of our aides and the weakest of our patients and the most burdened of our Sisters are so precious to Him. All life's riddles find their solution in the folly of the Cross. Only Love itself could make it so. O to make Love loved during this sacred season. How I anticipate this Lent. To sit at the foot of the Cross, and in the silence to hear each drop of Precious Blood fall into the chalice of my hands. To let not one drop go to waste. To drink the Chalice of Christ to the dregs, the Chalice that His precious lips have caressed He offers me. Thank you, Christ, O thank you!

Friday, March 8

This weekend Margot will tell me Jesus' wishes as regards joining the Institute. You told Him this step is only for His pleasure, didn't you? So whatever Margot says, I know He'll be happy, and then me, too.

Sunday, March 10

"I am resolved to know nothing but Jesus Christ, and Him crucified." As I sit here this evening, of all the goodies on our bulletin board these words shout Love to me. Happy, joyful Lent, my poor little soul. Love Him madly. Eternity won't be long enough.

It was such a thrill to see Anne-Marie once more, to greet Dorothy and Eileen, to meet Margot. After a wonderful weekend with these "Charlies," Father kindly brought me back to Good Sam. When I told Anne-Marie farewell, she said that he would tell me the news for which I've held my breath for days. So I could hardly wait to get into the car with him.

Then Christ spoke: "Little hobo, I love you. If you know this you will be thrilled at the news I speak through your dear Father Keith. You may not join the Secular Institute. Margot considers you yet very young and immature, and you ARE. You know that. And because I love you immeasurably I'll tell you also that Margot is wary because you're a handicapper. Now, that kinda shakes you up, doesn't it? Only lean hard, little one. You are so very weak not to stand erect under this. And yet because you must lean upon this shoulder that bears the burden of the world I love you dearly. How else might I caress you,

you who in your strength might find such delight in my creation that you wouldn't tire enough to let me play with your locks?

"Yes, child, they didn't let you speak. They sat to judge you behind closed doors. But who wishes to be bothered with the lisps of a silly little girl? How could you defend yourself? You don't even know yourself, for I am your true Self. And you know yet so little of Me. Lean here. And listen. I have eternity to teach you. Won't you stay?

"You know, you and this little go-cart are mighty heavy. And just think of all the days of recollection, retreats, etc., in which only mortals would be asked to care for you. I know you don't wish to hurt them. Please don't hurt Me by your tears. I love you. Need I say anything more? Convents can't take you, now even here your CP forbids you entrance. Keep going. I'm with you. Look around. See this great earth? It's your convent, your family, your heaven. Will you refuse this? What about your security? I just stepped on it? That's what this thing [*neck brace*] is around your neck, something to help you raise your head high. Look up. See. Great, glorious eternity. Run. I'm holding the Cross. You have nothing to bear. Only follow me. You can't see Easter's dawn for the big hill before you. It's called Calvary. I, too, have gone there. I am the WAY. Love your Jesus. He loves you."

Monday, March 11

See "Charlie's" picture hanging behind me, Mother? I'm so very happy to have it there; just one more reminder that I do have a family. Perhaps Jesus doesn't wish me to "belong" to any one specific group. He simply wants me to let Him BE wherever I am. In my selfish groping for security I often forget that I already possess Christ and am possessed by Him. He is happy? I am, too, O so happy because I'm falling into the bottomless chasm of Love with Christ.

Wednesday, March 13

"Things" seem so beautiful today. Must be the Sonshine you send your little hobo. To be just that, a little hobo for Jesus, like Jesus. Never to belong anywhere, so that I may bring Him everywhere. To have no earthly home so that heaven may shine in its true splendor. To be a mere child, scorned by the wise, so that Jesus will invite me to His open arms. To be a little child, tossed into the air by our heavenly Father, laughing with delight because I know that He will catch me. Father, I abandon myself into your hands, with boundless confidence, with the certainty of hope.

Thursday, March 14

Jean giggled at me today for my comment on Margot's refusal: "*Fiat*, darn it!" Because I'm your little child I know you'll hide the last part from the *fiat* you bring Our Father for me.

Monday, March 18

"Prayer and love are learned in the hour when prayer has become impossible and your heart has turned to stone." These words of Thomas Merton fell as dew upon my poor heart today. Mother, simply to wish to pray, to wish to love, is this not all Jesus asks? Forcing from His sacred Body the last breath of His mortal life, He threw Himself upon the bosom of His Father. And it was ended, the end of all ending, the Deed of God, eternal, magnificent act of Love Itself. O sacred hour today, when Christ whispered in recesses too deep to know waves tossed by a storm, "This is My Body." His Mass forever in a host ground from a thousand grains of selfishness. O Christ, be my Self!

Sunday, March 24 (Eve of the Feast of the Annunciation)

What were you doing on this evening nearly two thousand years ago, as all nature lay hushed in thrilling anticipation of the morrow? Were you washing dishes? Or maybe reading aloud at your mother's feet? "And His name shall be called Wonderful." Or maybe you'd already retired so that you might rise with the sun to greet the majesty of your God. Or maybe, just maybe, you were scratching a little love note to place where your mother would find it just before she retired. And you knew she would smile, so happiness lit your face as you wrote, "Goodnight, Mother."

Monday, March 25 (Feast of the Annunciation)

Christ! To what lowliness have You bowed. You've become as nothing. You have asked Mary to be the abode for a body that will be beaten, blood that will be spilled, a soul that will cry to God in the profound anguish of abandonment, divinity that will be stripped of all save the wood on which it will fling itself. "While all things were in quiet silence, Your almighty Word leapt down" to begin His Mass. May mine begin thus? Here I am, His little servant girl.

Everything today seemed to welcome Him. As I peeked out the chapel window, your blue shone in the sky. Little birds chirped a happy song. A clean, clear breeze gently kissed my cheek as it scurried by. I could see why Christ should love this earth so much as to make it His abode. I love it, too, and perhaps in happy freedom I can let Jesus enjoy all these wonders again. I could hardly explain today's lesson on the Holy Eucharist in quieting my heart that kept singing in awe at His promise to be with us always.

Thursday, March 28

My Mother, I come this evening to snuggle in your embrace. I'm so very tired. Everything seems so big. But I know it's just cause I'm a little one exhausted after playing in God's lovely world. With each little cross I feel myself stoop under the weight, and with every joy I hear the laughter nearly bursting in my heart. But now all is quiet and I'm here with you once again. And you nod and smile and understand.

Monday, April 1

Here's a droopy-eyed little one who's been sleeping in your arms practically all day. But still I like to write a little love note to you. Perhaps I can learn at times like these, when I'm apparently so useless, the lessons on "being" which my beloved Father Keith has been trying to teach me. I look at the shrine over there in the corner. Baby Jesus was "useless?" O to be your little one always!

Tuesday, April 2

Mother, it hurts. Not sure what, but guess muscle spasms. They plagued me last night and today. Seems that everything hurts. Just to relax. That's the answer, but I don't know how. I become a folded leaf, I stretch out upon the Cross, I kneel, I sit; poverty of positions, of strength but, please God, not of love. How else might we serve, me and my missionary, a little cross begging to be implanted in his Loving Heart? So this is Love! My heart knows it is.

Thursday, April 4

Christ let me come to Him this evening in the confessional. His Words? If I try to think of what His lips whispered they leave me. It is only their echo within the poverty of my heart that I hear. His message is full of sympathy and understanding. "Do you not know I love you?" I only desire to know. "Follow Me." He's going to die. I, too. He's going to bud forth from a stone tomb. I, too. Love does such things. I, too.

Friday, April 5

Mother, they say He loves you most. But today I watched Him. And He wounded your tender Heart again and again. I squeezed your hand, and as you stooped to hear a little one's whisper I asked you why such a thing should happen to God's Mother. You whispered, "Love does such things." And though my little mind could not grasp your words, my heart seemed satisfied and I couldn't seem to let you go.

Tuesday, April 9

There is much to tell you, yet I know you understand. So if I fall asleep in your arms tonight, for I'm O so tired, you won't forget to thank my Jesus for one second, will you? Goodnight, Mother. I'm so happy here, listening to the lullaby of your heart. I love you.

Monday, April 15

All day Holy Saturday in Elwood I went about singing in anxious anticipation. As I sat in church before Holy Mass that evening, I must have been kicking for joy. Father Keith came up to ask me if this was the night for renewal of my promises. Only to know that he knew made me happy. Sharing my joys with him simply increases them. Sometimes I think I'll burst if one more happiness comes along. But I don't; I just grow. Tell Jesus I'm His, beginning this very second and forever. Three golden links, Poverty, Chastity and Obedience, have bound me to Him. That's enough, for I am and must always be the least of His Little Sisters.

Easter morning I had the golden opportunity of speaking with Christ in the confessional. There my ears heard what my heart had heard the previous night. With this promise to Him it seems He wishes to make a promise to me, a promise of suffering. I know not how or why I feel that greater physical suffering will be my lot. Even in the confessional this was the main topic in His Easter message to me. *Accipio.* Tell Him, Mother, that I am ready to begin now.

Thursday, April 18

In chapel this evening everything seemed to speak to me of SILENCE. Mother, how very shamefully I've neglected this. I look at my Jesus, I look at you; I see that I've not let my Jesus live as He wishes in me. But a tremendous Lover reminds me how very far behind is each second of my life. He's interested only in NOW. He loves me NOW. I must love Him now, let Him live now. Gabriel awaits my *fiat* this second. He waits to fling it to God and in return bring divine beauty to a heap of dust. I beg God not to let me be guilty of divine abortion!

Sunday, April 21

What consolation I feel now, here in your arms, as you whisper that it is in my helplessness that Christ is best magnified. From a cold sepulcher comes eternal Life. And consolation of consolations, He loves me.

Monday, April 22

This afternoon I had the privilege of a wonderful visit with my dear Sister Jude and Sister Camilla. How I love them. This family you've given me, sometimes it seems just too wonderful. The world is mine. All creatures seem to shout God's sacred name to me. Ssshhh, my heart. Listen. Is there nothing that does not whisper of Jesus? Nothing.

Tuesday, April 23

Even though my eyelids are heavy and my mind dulled with fatigue, I must come to give you a goodnight kiss. And though soon I'll be apparently asleep, my heart longs to beat in union with yours so that not one second will pass without this incessant desire for my God.

Tuesday, April 30

Thank you, thank you, mother! A letter from [*Father Keith*] today. What baby sister could hope for something so wonderful? But I needn't hope for anything with a Mother such as you. Such loneliness that has been my companion of late. His letter only seemed to expose the wound I've tried so hard to hide for days. But I just can't hide it from you, Mother. Perhaps that's why I spent the day weeping in your arms. Mother, it does hurt much. I thought that time would ease the pain, but it is still my precious companion. Though I've tried hard to convince myself of my nonchalance, still my heart ever aches for Home. Thank God for this anguish. There is nothing else for me to offer. Only take this for one to whom you've given me, and I am happy. Joy of Christ, never will you not be mine.

Thursday, May 9 [Eve of her twenty-first birthday]

Please accept the orchid I place at the feet of my Mother this evening as I renew my Total Consecration to you. I thrill at the thought that you've given your poor little slave to my beloved Father Keith, and beg that I may always serve him with a Love that befits a gift from his Queen and Mother.

IN THE PRESENCE OF ALL THE HEAVENLY COURT I CHOOSE THEE THIS DAY FOR MY MOTHER AND MISTRESS. I DELIVER AND CONSE-CRATE TO THEE, AS THY SLAVE, MY BODY AND SOUL, MY GOODS, BOTH INTERIOR AND EXTE-RIOR, AND EVEN THE VALUE OF ALL MY GOOD ACTIONS, PAST, PRESENT AND FUTURE; LEAVING TO THEE THE ENTIRE AND FULL RIGHT OF DIS-POSING OF ME, AND ALL THAT BELONGS TO ME, WITHOUT EXCEPTION, ACCORDING TO THY GOOD PLEASURE, FOR THE GREATER GLORY OF GOD, IN TIME AND IN ETERNITY.

Marily in Love,
Little Virginia of Jesus, Vigil of May 10, 1963

Wednesday, May 15

Did you see your sleepy little one early this morning? It's always a little frustrating to break a shoestring. There are so many holes to lace in putting in another and it's so time-consuming and delicate for fingers that fumble. So I just told Jesus that was my first gift for my missionary today. Then the second string broke. I just sat there and giggled with Jesus. How great His sense of humor, and how very good that He shares it with me.

My beautiful Jean was here this evening for a couple hours. Had I not moved to Kokomo, God could never have sent me this beautiful soul to love. I'm so glad He gets His way. Tell Him to argue with me whenever necessary. I'm yet so little and fail to comprehend much. But He is wise and good and He loves me. This I know, as in the deepest confusion I whisper *fiat*.

Saturday, May 18

It's so good to be here in your arms right now to chatter about the little miracles with which Our Father has filled my way for the past three days. Though you come with me always, knowing I am too little to go alone, yet I see a smile on your lips as I visit with you each evening, and I kinda think you're pleased.

Thursday, May 21

Sing your lullaby vigorously tonight, Mother dear. Sing the *Magnificat* a little one is not able to lisp. Teach this heart, nearly bursting with Joy, to magnify our God.

Daddy came about noon last Sunday to take his little vagabond daughter to St. Meinrad's. Mother, I could hardly wait to write to you tonight to tell you all about our trip. Happy sight the confines of the Monastery were to the tired eyes of a little hobo.

And much happier the smile of our own Father Lucien as he bid us welcome. Praised be God, Who made such a great man as he. When Daddy had gone to bed, Father and I chatted a few minutes. He told me how he remembered the tears I gave him one day, the day I received crushing news from the Sisters of the Lamb of God. A confirmation of *Amicitia* in tears and laughter. Yes, he loved me as Jesus

With Father Lucien Duesing, O.S.B., during her first visit to St. Meinrad Archabbey, May 1963

loves me, not in spite of my weakness but BECAUSE of it. Eternal the debt of gratitude for Love from Love.

Immeasurable gifts of wisdom and kindness, of precious time and of Love did Father Lucien shower upon me during our visit. Never must there be goodbyes, but eternal greetings in Christ. *Deo gratias!*

Friday, May 31

I'm tired, Mother, O so tired and Homesick. How I long to be with my Jesus. Please ask Him to forgive such selfish longings. Of course, I shall wait till the end of the world and die a thousand martyrdoms if He wishes. Every day is a little martyrdom; I'm happy because I know my Jesus is eternally happy. That is enough. And I know that a Mother such as mine never forgets her poor little child so far from Home. "All the way to Heaven is Heaven." Yes, I know.

There was time this afternoon to have made my visit to Jesus. But though the spirit was willing, I couldn't seem to drag my poor frame from its little heap here on the floor. I was so grateful to be able to crawl to our record player to put on the wonderful disc Father Lucien gave us. Nothing but songs of you for my happy heart to sing on your feast day. From your *fiat* to your *Magnificat*, I long to reproduce the songs you sang to Jesus so that He might feel at home with me. Please teach me to sing.

Monday, June 3

The one letter I wrote this morning, with so much effort, I now see that I can't mail because I've lost the address. I just tore the letter up and laughed as I threw it in the wastepaper basket. So much time and strength and Love on one worthless piece of paper to be burned. Jesus must have read it, though. All things are so passing, yet so important, because Jesus loves me.

Thursday, June 6

Let me never be greedy, never alarmed to recognize my poverty in the midst of true lovers. Let me be satisfied with just what Jesus sends, never to wish that another's sanctity may be mine, wishing only to love Him with all the Love capable of filling one tiny heart. To be the least in the kingdom of heaven, the most forgotten of all His toys, but only to be His. As He wishes.

Friday, June 7

Perhaps one day I shall enter the depths of Love where silence reigns. Perhaps. But as yet there is music everywhere. Jesus must wish it that way; I, too. His happiness is mine. Just to be there at His feet. He is so silent, so useless it seems. And a little sister pours her uselessness at His feet. Only He could be delighted with such a gift. To delight Him is my sole delight.

Sunday, June 9

How this little vagabond longs for her Home. Let this yearning but increase the Fire of divine Love. One day, O sweet hope, I shall be consumed. Then I shall be in Love forever. My God, in the depths of my nothingness I long for Thee, and in this very longing I am plunged even deeper into Thee! I believe; please help my disbelief.

Tuesday, June 11

I rest here in you arms tonight, arms that cradled me each second of this day. Such a special day it's been resting here in your embrace. How tightly you held me here. O Mother, never let me go. Sometimes I felt the power of your love, others the tenderness. My arms, my legs, my back and neck, this incessant ache. Is it pain as I feel it or a heartache? I know not. I am so very Homesick, yet even in this exile I am cradled within my Mother's arms. Sometimes I can hardly tell if pain hurts. It matters little. I'm Maryly in LOVE because I'm in your arms. That is enough.

Wednesday, June 12

We got the brochure on the Little Brothers in today's mail. It's such a treat. I do love my universal family. The world is mine because I am Jesus'. I asked for a little corner; He offers a world, a universe and finally a celestial Home. Love does such things.

Thursday, June 13

Mother of Jesus, you whose very flesh and blood formed the Sacred Humanity that would house your God, how can arms that cradled Divinity now stretch out to me? Perhaps I shall never understand. Love does such things. O when will I begin to fathom God? I know only what you tell me of Him. I love to hear of Him. When your lips are silent, your very heart whispers JESUS with each beat.

Tuesday, June 18

Our dear Jean came this evening. Such joy! O if only I

could love LOVE. It's terrible to have nothing to give in return for GOD. I must learn to be still, to be satisfied to be so deficient, to desire to be the least even in Virtues if Jesus wishes. Just to be little, to be nothing, and in the contrast my brothers and sisters will see the Majesty of God.

four

---

*T*hese months mark a pivotal time in Virginia's life. She is forced to deal with a decline in physical strength. She does so by attempting time and again to abandon the wheelchair in favor of crutches. She comes to realize that her desire to walk — even after Dr. Jahns warns her to cease the practice — is a temptation against her vocation, a wish to "sport her independence," contrary to the Will of God. Her loss of strength coincides with a growing spiritual aridity, and she comes to understand that her vocation is to involve intense suffering. Her attitude toward nighttime changes. Rather than dreading the long, solitary hours, she welcomes them as time to keep precious vigil with the Lord. There is also a growing awareness that her life, in union with the redemptive sacrifice of Jesus, has universal implications. Virginia recounts her many excursions undertaken in the name of her vocation as "God's little hobo." She comes to accept this vocation so wholeheartedly that she informs Mother Madeleine that she is no longer interested in becoming a Sister. She makes two trips to Gary, Indiana, and a second trip to St. Meinrad's, at which time she meets Father Eugene Ward. Her work in the Jesus-Caritas movement continues to bear fruit. She renews her vows on August 15th, and again on December 8th. She writes: "My heart must be His Calvary. He must feel free to forge His Holy Cross into its depths."

✝
LOVE

Thursday, June 20, 1963

All morning I waited to go with our friends to their get-together, but no one came. Not wishing to begin a letter only to quit, I sat reading the booklet on our Little Brothers. Time well spent with my "Charlie" family. How I love any word from any of them. Again this evening I was told that someone would be here for me between seven and seven-thirty. But no one came. So what with the rest I had to take this afternoon, you see what a *useless* day I've spent. But each second was with my Jesus. Only He knows the value of things we do or do not do. Please help me learn to be His little nothing. Let others forget me, "disappoint" me, and if I only know that Jesus is not disappointed in me that is enough. How can I ever be disappointed if He is my Everything?

Sunday, July 7

Always and everywhere you seem to be lovingly teaching me of your little Child. O how you yearn for me to become like your Love. Mother, I've disappointed you so often. O to never hurt you again. I see you often at the Thirteenth Station. You hold a lifeless Body and adore a living Soul. I never wish to bring you the torment of gazing at me and finding my soul lifeless. Never!

Thursday, July 11

A letter from Elwood today! Thank you, Mother dear. It meant much to hear from Anne; very, very much. How I've longed to hear from SOME "Charlie." As Anne, "Sometimes I feel my desert is overwhelming." Dryness more petrifying; even all the tears I've shed can't begin to moisten it. Thank

God that I may share so very much with Brother Charles. He longed for the Holy Family of Nazareth, and in his longing he was alone. Truly he has let me imitate him all the more by being nothing "official" in his family. A little nothing. That is enough for Jesus? Then if He's happy, I, too.

Friday, July 12

Please help me to learn your prompt and unquestioning obedience to the Will of the Father, you who know just what Jesus would do. Somehow God will be glorified as others discover my own nothingness, my terrible weaknesses and failures. They will know what is NOT He. Then lead them on, Mother dear, to be perfect as He is perfect, with His very Perfection. This I beg for all those of my family, for the world.

Sunday, July 14

How near was He today, making His delightful Presence known to me, strengthening me for yet other days when I shall go in search of Him and become lost in the milling crowds, when my wretchedness shall blind me to His Presence, when feebly I trudge on following Him I know not where, when our rendezvous leads us to Calvary. I shall go on, for I shall remember today. He was so near.

Tuesday, July 16

We weren't permitted to attend Holy Mass this morning, for Father Kohne felt so badly. But Jesus came to be with us all day. My heart must be His Calvary. He must feel free to forge His Holy Cross into its depths. No one ever felt its pain or triumph more than you. Because you are the Mother of Sorrows, you have become the Mother of the Blessed. You are mine, too, by some prodigality of Almighty Goodness. Never shall I understand this happiness. But it is mine.

Wednesday, July 17

Today is Sister Alexis' feast day. How I love her. Do you see her each morning as we prepare to go down to Holy Mass in the elevator? She looks around to be sure I'm coming, then smiles really wide and almost sings, "Good morning, Teresa!" At least it's music to my heart. She's constantly reminding Sister Aquinas not to forget to take care of the "child." Guess she really worried about me when I was in Gary. And when I didn't show for Holy Mass on Sunday she was truly alarmed. She's a darling. Please, Mother, take care of her as she does of me. And let the world know what she knows, that I am but a little one. Only my love must be great. Jesus-Love.

Today is Sister Camilla's feast day. Just had to remind you, Mother. I love to remind you of all my brothers and sisters in Love. You seem so pleased at the mere thought of them. It's such a thrill to come to you with requests for my brothers and sisters, to see your smile and know that I never ask for them in vain. I, too, wish to please you thus, I, their very little sister. Perhaps you can love me much because I am the least, the least in Love, and yet I desire to please you. Somehow I think that my desire is sufficient. With Jesus I've come to do the Will of the Father. And what would I want more than it be accomplished? Teach me the complete dependence and total surrender of your *fiat*.

Saturday, July 20

Please remind me often of my dear brother "Charlie," of his consuming love of the Holy Eucharist and Holy Mass, of the terrible deprivation he endured in not being able to offer the Holy Sacrifice. It's wonderful that he permits the very least of his Little Sisters to join her suffering to his. It seems he's bringing me ever closer to the life that was his, the life of Jesus of Nazareth. I long for Nazareth, and in this longing I possess it. Nazareth was a long period of yearning for my Jesus. How often He must have sighed that His Hour hadn't come yet.

How many nights He lay there gazing heavenward to the bosom of the Father. Perhaps He got very Homesick. Yes, Mother, Jesus knows, and lives. Jesus-Caritas!

Monday, July 29

How happy is your little one to be here with you once more. All is quiet. From our record player soar soft notes of your *Magnificat*. And from my heart a song blends with it as you sing a goodnight song to your Jesus.

Julie came for just a little while late Tuesday night. She told us a little about the "Charlies'" retreat in Montreal. Such precious morsels to be shared. Please forgive me for the heartburn after Julie left. If I would feed on Jesus and Him alone I would not experience such distress. But once again my longing to join the Secular Institute was enflamed. And yet in the brilliance of those fires I could well see that Jesus did not will it, nor I. I know not how I could want something so intensely and yet not want it all at the same time. Another paradox solved only in Love. Ask Jesus to make me a good little hobo. You will care for crippled "Charlies," too, I know. Only let us never be handicapped in Love.

Tuesday, July 30

A day alone with Jesus, doing the little routine things with HIM we cannot do in the divine milieu. It was such a happy day, filled with silence and smiles, with Jesus, with Love. Can I somehow express sufficient gratitude? You can, Mother. Please sing to Him the ditties that fill my heart.

Friday, August 9

So much a little one wishes to share with her beautiful Mother this evening. Can we sit here late this evening, just you and I, speaking of Jesus and His lovers, not a word that doesn't secretly whisper His sweet Name? Mother, I just knew you'd stay up with me. Let me snuggle yet closer. The evening is warm, everything a bit sticky, but in Your embrace is all my refreshment. Springtime is always in the eyes of my Mother.

I must not have been a very pretty little one on Wednesday morning. All night I got to watch with Jesus; sleep dared not disturb Us. I could hardly breathe, only little short, quick breaths, and such pain. I kept wishing that Jesus would take me. But no, only He could know how unworthy I remain to stand before Him. My little ones yet cry for help. How could I wish to meet Him without having mothered these? No, I must remain to love these He gives me, the world. I may be weary, but I must not sleep, not yet.

All day Thursday you seemed to whisper secrets from one co-missionary to another. There are those who envy this little hobo's carefree life, those who know not Jesus' little vagabond. O such responsibility is mine. It scares me, fills me with joy, chokes me, thrills me, makes me stagger under the load, only to fall into the strong embrace of my God. Sometimes I feel that I cannot go on, that I MUST rest, that such exhaustion would merely appear as indifference to those I go to love. But Jesus invites me elsewhere. And with His strength I need never refuse. Somehow His Love must shine through this fatigue. And this smile must reflect His Joy and Life.

Thank God that I am so tired this evening. I wish that I might travel to the ends of the earth, till the end of time, to love Jesus and make Him loved. Please never forget your wandering little one in her exile. Someday soon I shall come Home to you forever. So soon. My God, let not this longing be in vain!

Saturday, August 10

Today seemed to be one of big adjustments. It's like I've just moved to Good Sam. Everything seems strange. The cries, the angry words that reached me in chapel seemed to cut twice as deep. Thank God for leading His little one so many places to love Him. O to remain almost invisible among man. Jesus knows I'm here; that is enough.

Mary Romack called just as we were finishing supper this evening. I grow a little frightened now and then when my little ones come to me for words of Divine Wisdom. Truly they could never realize just how stupid I am. But that's all right, for I beg Jesus to speak. And I am filled with confidence. It seems so easy to speak the Love within the poverty of my heart. To hear of the joy with which these counsels are received convinces me that Jesus lives today. May He live and love eternally in His little Virginia!

Sunday, August 11

See our new August bulletin board? How my heart beats as the 15th approaches. "Since you gave my heart away. . . ." Thus the letters read this month. So much have you given your little child since that day one year ago, *because* of that day. Guess those were the first words with which Father Keith acknowledged our gift. Remember? I thanked him for the conference on poverty that had so deeply moved me. And his gracious reply rang sweet and loud, "Many wonderful things have been happening since you gave your heart away." He did realize the significance of your gift to him! Never shall I forget that moment, that Love. Never do I wish to lose the beauty of that eternal moment during the Holy Sacrifice when you told me you were giving me to be his. Little did I understand, but I heard your gentle voice. Even yet I cannot comprehend this joyous Love that binds a priest and a cripple. It isn't important to understand. *Accipio.*

Tuesday, August 13

My little ones wait anxiously for letters, and I can send them so few. Mother, please care for them. I am no woman, merely a little one myself, a little one crying their tears.

Friday, August 16

It's so good to be here with you this evening, my beautiful Mother. So good to rest here on a heart whose incessant murmurings whisper Jesus' name. This is the only song I need learn to sing.

The desert where Jesus led me last Wednesday was most unique, a place apart in the midst of noisy activities. Just as I'd gone to be with Him in the Blessed Sacrament, He sent me out to the telephone to speak with Myrna. Vagabond assignment, pack quick 'cause We're going to Myrna's. For an instant I nearly argued. It seemed there should be one day alone with Him now and then. But no, never can I be with Him alone. So many little ones follow Him everywhere, and to wish to take Him from them or them from Him is to ask Him to leave these who delight Him so. Surely you never asked Him to come aside from them. Nor I. Ask Him to pardon the silly impulses that escape the arid depths of my heart.

Jesus is good to let me see Our little sister Myrna so often. I know this privilege is granted to few. Perhaps it is mine to make me more aware of my own unworthiness. Sometimes I think Jesus finds the deserts of our hearts merely to show us that He is the Master of the impossible, for even there He can make Love's blossoms burst forth in sweet fragrance.

You must always show me the way to Calvary. I wander off on paths that smell of sweet flowers and sing with little birds and sparkle with rainbows. And then I get lost. I can't find Jesus, for this wasn't His way, nor yours. Then your voice calls. I look up to see a Cross. It's not beautiful. I wish to run the other way. But you call gently, patiently, passionately. Jesus is the Way. And He hangs on the Cross. O please keep calling. And tell Him I'm coming, so slowly; He's waiting so patiently. If only I might run!

Sunday, August 18

If these letters to you were as beautiful as "Brother Charles" writings, surely they would be so pleasing to Jesus. I don't pretend to be a hermit as "Charlie," nor even to meditate. I simply come to be with you at the end of the day. That's all. If I am not beautiful like your other children, perhaps the shades of dusk will mercifully hide my ugliness. Your eyes see far beyond that ugliness. So far beyond that Christ fills your dreams. Christ, Who wishes to inebriate me that I, too, might bring you happiness as He does. Bring Him, Mother, to fill the dark, damp, stony cavern of my heart, that it may be as dear to you as the cave in which you first laid Him.

It's time to say goodnight now, Mother, and I love you, and to press your Jesus close in this silence and adore.

Monday, August 19

O to go to God in childlike simplicity. To rush to Him, forgetting my ugly nakedness, remembering His mercy, His omnipotence, His majesty, His Love: eternal, inexhaustible Love. Only to be there in His Sacred Presence, annihilated, a little nothing. All silly concern about how I must pray or sing, to think or act, must vanish. To be with Him is all that matters. It's kinda dumb to dictate to Him what I wish Our visit to be. I don't do this to other friends. And He doesn't do this to me. He is Kindness. I love to be with Him, for when I find Him there I find the world and heaven and all things.

Tuesday, August 20

Today has seemed like a bit of Christmas somehow. Jesus, so little and so mighty, resting in the hearts of all men, in my poor heart. It was hard to suppress Christmas carols during my hour with Jesus. I didn't. Whatever fills my heart I spill at His feet. There is nothing else to do when I'm there with Him. It's useless to pretend that I'm a great contemplative, that I am filled with beautiful thoughts of Him. He knows the selfish designs of my heart. Sometimes to give Him only what is mine is painful. But He accepts graciously and offers to God the Father what is His.

Sometimes it's easy to imagine what love and devotion I would have brought to the crèche where you and your almighty Infant were sheltered. But you lay Him daily in our souls. And daily I fail to recognize Him. And you extend once more that timeless invitation, "O come let us adore Him!" My love is my greatest handicap, but I am coming. Please keep calling me.

Monday, September 2

Truly it IS good for me to be here, Mother dear, alone with you and the world and Heaven. But alone, His alone, because you give me to Jesus.

Thoughts and prayers and Love are surging in my heart, in my mind, too mingled and exalted and simple to narrow to these little pages. And yet I wish to write to you. Why? I do not know. Yet I know that you love me, and that is sufficient.

Wednesday morning, August 21st, I awoke to God's morning and — confusion. The strange sensation of finding all my things topsy-turvy, myself not yet dressed, my packing not begun, such a lost feeling, unfamiliar. And yet it was good, I know. Only a preview of what the next two weeks would bring. It seems that during that time all was taken from me. My prayer life was gone. My Short Breviary never completed one day. Rosaries impossible to squeeze in. Holy Mass and Communion such a rarity that when I did attend I became so choked up with joy I could not read from my Missal nor hardly follow the prayers, only sit and marvel that I was really there. Such a desert, such a magnificently barren desert. Such prayer and love within a heart devoid of such. O immensity of divine Love, consume one devoid of all save nothingness! If only there were only nothingness here. But no, there is wretched sinfulness. Mine to give: Poverty of self.

Before Jesus came to us that morning, He seemed to whisper again and again, "Ask, and you shall receive." Ask from the depths of humility. In your hesitation you seem to doubt my Love. Believe, and ask." My God, I ask, I beg, that the world be consumed in the flames of Divine Love. I can think of no more exalted request, nor one that You must be more anxious to accomplish. Yet it seems that if I continue to smother the spark of your Love in my heart I have no right to ask this of You. And still I ask, in confidence.

Thursday I had a day in the desert. I got to sing aloud all my Short Breviary. And only Love heard. Then a few practice rounds on the crutches. Not bad. I have been secretly practicing lately. It's so easy to spend myself on them. And I felt that day that I haven't yet accepted this handicap. True, I feel so good at present. But it's hard to convince myself that I'm not cured. Mediocrity is a staggering cross at times. You see, I was trying to walk alone for a minute. Just wishing, hoping in this recent strength. But my legs give out. I fall. My back is pulled. It aches. Jesus will show me how to learn to accept all the Simons in my life graciously instead of sporting my independence.

Father Keith brought me back to Good Sam this morning. Thank you for letting me be with him once more, to tell him something of the inexpressible sorrow that fills my heart. And to receive his gentle reprimands. But please help me thank Jesus most of all for His Absolution when I'd returned to my corner. Now I go in Peace and Simplicity, in Jesus' Love. May my little brother go likewise. I know we go together.

Tuesday, September 3

See our new September bulletin board? That little prayer at the bottom must become mine: "Lord, fill my mouth with worthwhile stuff, and nudge me when I've said enough."

Mother, I want to become like you, a woman wrapped in silence, a woman in love, and yet it seems I go further and further from this ideal. O such painful failure. And yet if this mere desire pleases Jesus, that is enough.

Wednesday, September 4

As we were waiting for Jesus in Holy Communion this morning, it seemed days passed. But He didn't come. How painful to leave chapel, after expecting Him for so long. A short pain and a long joy, for here He is buried forever in the poverty of my heart. And it sings. I remembered something Father Keith wrote to me last year at Christmas time: "May Christ never have to wait for you." Yes, Mother, that is how you were that eternal day. Alone, waiting, the doors of your heart opened joyously, and Love entered to stay. Yes, He came this morning, so silently I hardly noticed. But I heard His Breath, and smiled.

Monday, September 9

This morning I heard you whisper so sweetly, so clearly, "Love expects all things." You seemed to repeat it endlessly. You know how hard it is for my poor heart to understand. But you never tire. You're such a patient Mother. To hesitate with a request is to doubt Love, to deny God the opportunity to once more show me His tremendous Love. He loves to grant our worthy requests, and it seems the greater their impossibility, the more hurriedly He wishes to accomplish them. Otherwise, how dare I beg Him to dwell within my heart?

Wednesday, September 11

This morning, when Jesus was so close, when the thought of Him quickened my poor heart, He whispered to His little hobo, "Many, many have desired to hold What you hold." O Mother, to hold Him for them, to love Him for them, to love them for Him! And somehow to bear Him for them, for the world. And to be in labor until He is known and loved by all! Somehow. You are my Mother. You know the Way.

Wednesday, September 18

Thoughts of St. Meinrad's have permeated all my joys today. Father Lucien's reminder that the world is my HOME, and Meinrad's special rank, has been a tremendous consolation. I've needed this for so long, this special spot. When my precious Velma's home ceased to be this to me I became so confused without an earthly "somewhere." Just to know that it is there waiting for me, and a loved one, a big brother, waits too, is enough. Truly there is never a need, silly as might be the hobo's desires, that Divine Providence does not immediately supply.

It is once more time for rest. Nights are so long and dark and confusing. But to remember sitting at Jesus' feet and to hear once more His words of consolation is enough. I go to keep a rendezvous.

Thursday, September 19

We got to have a get-together at Jean's this morning. It was such a treat, had been so long since we'd been there. Jean was there, and Love, and all was beautiful. The bond between Jean and me seems to grow constantly to depths too deep for even my desires. Each time I am with her there are discoveries, and Christ. To have a dear one such as she here in Kokomo is a dream only Divine Love could have fashioned, and I may only surrender my joy to God and weep that my Love is yet so shallow.

Saturday, September 21

O these bitter temptations of late! So painful, so strong. Never has Satan played upon my handicap so. He calls it laziness. This evening I tried to say Stations on my feet. Mother, even Jesus needed aid, yet I was trying to sport my "independence" in His Sacred Presence. My legs crumbled thrice, my back and head throbbed, and at last I was nailed to this cross and in joy cried, "Into Thy hands I commend myself." *Accipio*!

Tuesday, September 24

Our new sister arrived this afternoon, her room right next to where I sleep upstairs. My Jesus, mercy! She lies there with only animal instincts left. She tears the clothes and blankets from her, trying to find enough strength to shred them. She yells out continually but her words are incoherent. O my poor sister! My poor family here, throughout the world. Gentle Mother, never forget that we are your little ones. Please never forget. Without you my tears would be incessant. But you are beautiful, and with you I shall always smile, you the Queen of Martyrs and the happiest of all women.

Thursday, September 26

When I was sitting with Jesus at noon today, there were two little candles burning, almost consumed. They were so pretty, almost doing a ballet for Jesus at times, and then again glowing in the silence of Love. One burned tall and courageous; the other was leaning far to one side. Yet I watched the first die in peace and silence. And the second burned on. Jesus and I watched it together. And we giggled. For that little flame was apparently gone so often, but then it would hold its head high once more. When an aide came for me it was still peeking over the top of the candlestick.

Sunday, October 6 [After a visit to St. Meinrad's]

Greetings, beautiful Mother. Truly it is good for us to be here. I love you; I love to be with you, to know that you are mine and I am yours and the world's, that God is great and He is ours and we are nothing yet in Him all things to all men. And He loves us. O insurmountable mystery. HE LOVES US!

It's so difficult to begin to tell you of this past week. I seem to ramble on and on in my thoughts, in a circle of which Divine Love is the center. But you seem to smile from the depths of your Immaculate Heart, condescending to listen to your poor little one, understanding what she does not. Yet in the brilliance of your smile I find clarity. Mother, I am so happy Jesus gave you to me and me to you. Lord, I am not worthy! I hurt you by being so very far from what Jesus is. Yet you wait, you look into my heart and wait to find the living Christ. Please, Jesus, live here today.

I HAVE MET FATHER EUGENE, and I have known Christ as I have never known Him before. He lives forever, and my soul remembers His Face. Now this exile can never be dark. His memory is sweetness. Wordless, God-filled communications permeated our moments together, apart, our joyous meetings, our quiet partings, our eternal memories until we shall one day realize that these are no longer memories but incessant realities. O Mother, words would but diminish, mar, this experience. Yet you know Christ — you understand.

Now here I am at Good Sam for a little while. And somehow I am very happy to be here, to be anywhere in Love. These have been beautiful days. Yet now is the time to see true beauty. Now is the time to share Love with all my poor brothers and sisters. God is here in the Eternal Present. It is time to rest, but Love burns brightly, and this retreat is immortal. I love. . .

Monday, October 7

There are O so many mysteries to take and ponder within the poverty of my heart, Mother dear. All day I have remembered, and smiled, and watched their beauty grow yet more radiant in Almighty God's eternal NOW.

Wednesday, October 9

My missionary arrived at eight-thirty this morning. And for the first time in a year we journeyed to the clinic together. Yes,

Virginia and Father Keith getting ready for a trip

God is good. Many have desired to possess what God begs me to accept graciously. Yes, I know. And responsibility, I know this, too. My God-clad brother spoke words his poor little missionary could not understand. But in my heart I keep them till one day I shall see, and understand.

Miss Slo gave me another cervical collar, even more efficient than the first. Thank God for such a blessing. She also had another chair built for me, and promised an even more appropriate one come December. She is even trying to find me a craft to occupy my spare time, though I know not what THAT is. But the thought is beautiful enough.

On the way home, Father and I rode through the midnight silence, peering at the dancing stars; two very tired pilgrims on our way to Eternity. Through my heart rushed a painful yet joyous echo. O Lord, I am not worthy! May the WORD be his; may he forget my babble.

Friday, October 11

Mother! If there were a more beautiful title fashioned by the heart of your children, how anxiously would I whisper it, sing it, shout it, type it in these little love notes to you. But surely the name Jesus gave you must please you most. O Mother of Love, bending to mother a sinner, you are beautiful!

A letter from Father Lucien! I just knew it would come soon, filled with strength and refreshment. "You know that you are a member of our community now — because we are all hobos in this temporary world of ours, and you know where we live and you know where the Guest House is. So please do direct your thoughts and prayers to us all the time, and please direct yourself to us any time." Mother, how gently this falls upon the weeping heart of a child in exile.

Saturday, October 12

So long did we sit anxiously waiting in chapel this morning. But we were forgotten. No priest came to feed us poor little sheep. The hours of waiting seemed so endless. As often as my poor body would permit I looked upon my crucified Love. And when my facial muscles were contorted in pain, even then I know that He could see a smile. Miss Slo told Father Keith, 'She should have NO pain." Perhaps she forgot my Bridegroom. The little moans, the spasms, the constant stabs in my right hip area, deep breaths caught hurriedly now and then, these betrayed my pain. But Jesus hung in silence. God forgive my cowardice! Now all is quiet. And a short pain is eternal Joy.

Monday, October 28

How filled with tender caresses was my Beloved today. He let me spend my entire hour with Him sitting on the floor before His little golden shelter, so close, so indescribably close. There is nowhere He doesn't seek to embrace us, this tremendous Lover of men. He said again and again and again today, "You are nothing. Nothing! And I am yours, your Jesus, your Love, your All." My God, I believe! O please strengthen the weakness of my Faith. In the splendor of His Presence we become stripped of all that we may become radiant with Truth, radiant with Christ. "No, not I." Live, Jesus, and love.

Friday, November 1

My Beloved at last called me to speak to Him for a few minutes in the confessional last night. How sweet His invitation. I hadn't had this privilege for two months. I know, Mother, it seems a tragic length of time. But I wish to take always what He sends. And besides, I know of your tender care. With what confidence may I fly to God, knowing all I need to serve Him is mine. So many argue that I must learn to do "my part." But I have no part. I am His little nothing. O to never spoil the beautiful designs of Divine Providence by my silly schemes.

Sunday, November 3

Mother, somehow tell Jesus of my gratitude that He should invite me to die with Him in two Holy Masses today. There at your feet I once more sang aloud the *Magnificat* my heart always hears you humming. Such a poor little heart cannot contain all this joy, but must often spill forth its song. Perhaps one day my joys will reach its depths, where I shall love in mighty Silence, pondering all things there. Perhaps. But now I remain but your little child, so noisy, yet to be Jesus' is enough. Whether He should let me become a beautiful woman like you or remain such a child, falling often, yet bouncing right up to run on to a rendezvous with Him, matters little.

Tuesday, November 5

My Beloved once more tried to silence the useless murmurings of my silly heart when He came today. O divine patience! How often I rebuke myself, my laziness, my uselessness. How often I attempt strutting about in independence, only to fall flat on my face, to remember Dr. Jahns's warnings about such caprices. My weak legs ache, and my back and my neck shoot pain through my head, and my heart pounds and my breathing comes is gasps. Then I return to my wheels, God's own gift to me. Mother, let me not refuse them, nor anything He sends. How often He must sigh in disappointment. But you are my Queen, my Mother, and I am but a wee beginner. So all becomes tinted in golden hope. I fling myself into your arms tonight in abandonment and utter confidence.

Thursday, November 7

This is the last evening I may write to you from this little corner, for Jesus' little hobo must move on. I've loved it here, Mother, you know that. So accessible to those who come to visit, the silence, the homey atmosphere Our Father planted in this wee little spot. But now I become more and more a Little Sister, as "Charlie" wishes, for I must spend the entire day and night on third now. My new corner is right next to the bathroom, and the spot where the aides smoke and visit. The patients' constant cries won't escape me now. O thank God. I know this little sister has been too sheltered. Now there will be no privacy such as I in my selfishness have loved. For the aides always wish to chat, or simply to satisfy their curiosity as to what a little handicapper does with her time. Once more my bulging knapsack must be tidied. I cannot say, "There is no longer room for me in my own house," for that has never been my own. But in the secrecy of my heart, perhaps, I have cluttered many little corners with frivolous baggage. Now help me to dispose of all that is not Jesus so that I may run to Him in childlike freedom. And please thank Him for me.

Friday, November 8

Good evening, Mother dear. Don't you think the new little corner is lovely? Please tell our Father I'm so pleased with it, so thrilled. How could I have been otherwise when eternal

Kindness was planning this for me? Ask Him to forgive my for-getfulness. I should have known, I His own little hobo. It's been a rather long day, what with all the moving, so I'll just curl up here in your arms now. I'm glad you're here!

Tuesday, November 12

So often I've permitted the murmurings of others to dis-turb the depth of Love in my heart. But now such surface dis-turbances are so insignificant, SO false. It is HE I love, more and more deeply. O precious discovery of this day, *Deo gratias*.

Wednesday, November 13

Hello, Mother. I love this time when all else has been put away for the night and my last delightful pecking is to you. Most of my brothers and sisters have gone to sleep, and the night's noises consist of trucks rumbling by and the purr of Anita, except when I touch her keys to tell you goodnight and of my love. Fatigue has kinda dulled my brain, and though my heart sings, my thoughts ramble on and it's hard to put them on paper. But we're here together, so nothing else matters. Jesus is in our midst, but how dare I speak to you of Him? Still you listen. O my precious Mother!

Friday, November 15

Mother dear, there are no words to type this evening. It is enough to be here with you, to know that you are here and that you love the little and the poor.

Friday night; Jesus has been placed in the tomb. In other faces I read misery, loneliness, fear. Yet your face is peace to my heart and a smile upon my lips. For you know something they've forgotten, and with the secret your heart alone has claimed for its own, you shield me from loneliness forever. I'm glad you're here and I wait with you.

Wednesday, November 20

This morning, my head having fallen thrice here on Anita in tired nothingness, Jean and Mary's smiling faces peeped in the door. Such a pretty sight to enliven my heart. We were soon whisking to Lou's house to sip coffee together with Jesus, His Presence yet more a reality to us each time we gather in His Holy Name. Yes, in His strength I can do all things. Alone I might have declined the invitation this morning. But the eagerness of His Love to be with those dear ones quickened my poor heart, and joyously did I go there with Him. Then, when we got back to Good Sam, We scooched to Our little corner to sleep a sweet slumber. All is sweet when He has made us His own, and we remember our Beloved.

Thursday, November 21

This evening I am exhausted. I wish to be alone here in our little corner. I long to keep watch this Thursday night. Yet I feel completely drained, even unable to read these insensible words I must be typing to you right now. I must close. My eyes already are closing. This Way has drained my all. You understand, Mother, much better than I. Come, let us seek rest that tomorrow we may be strong once more to seek Him. In joyous longing we anticipate His Resurrection. Come, Jesus!

Sunday, December 1

Father Keith called me Friday evening. My precious director gave me permission to renew my promises to Jesus on the feast of your Immaculate Conception, only one week from today. It will be my second anniversary. Please flee from me all thoughts of time, that I may live in the Eternity of the Blessed Trinity.

Saturday night, after all the others were in bed, I watched with Jesus as His new year came upon us. It is good to be here, to go to chapel and once more be there alone with Jesus, and yet the world. May this be the happiest of all the new years of grace our world has known. How good to be with Him, to make the first word my heart and my lips and my pencil utter in this thrilling cycle of Holy Mother Church: JESUS.

Monday, December 2

All day my precious little brother "Charlie" has been so near. Though yesterday was actually the anniversary of his death, I got the dates confused. But little did it matter in God's eternal Present. "Live today as if you shall die a martyr's death." Prepare yourself to be thrown upon the dirt, the sand of the desert, by those you love, your friends; your clothing shredded, your throat parched, your entire life a succession of failures, all your plans as his, mere bits of paper, a total failure. This, my soul, is your greatest hope, your true success story.

Tuesday, December 3

Precious Mother, in the silent waiting of Holy Mother Church, teach me to mother Christ in the silences of my own heart, in depths I've not as yet fathomed. During this joyous waiting, while His entire Church becomes pregnant with Him, give me your own Immaculate Heart with which to adore the Incarnate Word yet but a Whisper, longing for His cry to pierce this night with brilliance.

Wednesday, December 4

My Jesus didn't rest upon my tongue this morning. How I longed to receive Him into my yearning, but He sent me rather to find Him where four little sisters gathered in His Name. How glorious the embrace after a search. Teach me, Mother, to search constantly, untiringly, till at last my heart is eased at the sound of His Voice in every temple, every human soul.

Sunday, December 8

Good evening, precious Mother, spotless joy of almighty God and of all little ones who claim you for their own. I am yours; I am His; I am Father Keith's; I am the little sister of all; most of all, I am Nothing. My poor heart cannot be quiet tonight, yet it knows not what to say. I sit here in the Presence of God and seem to disappear and realize that only when I am no more shall I be satisfied. I cannot sing, nor pray, nor meditate. Nor can I even BE what I wish to be for Jesus. Yet this is enough, this darkness, and a Star that leads across the desert.

Thursday evening Jesus gently beckoned that I might speak with Him. Patiently He stilled my concerns, patiently must I learn your *fiat*. Strange that there in the confessional that evening, my chat with Jesus completed, I should ask Father Keith to pray for me today. I've never asked prayers of him; always my life is FOR him. But he let me know he doesn't forget by a promise to pray for me, "especially" today. And the power of those prayers has penetrated today into depths I'd not yet fathomed. Then he sent me forth in Peace to prepare for this day our God has made for us.

Last night I hardly wished to sleep. My longing for today [*the day Virginia was to renew her vows*] was so intense. Yes, even in my yearning do I discover possession of the Desired of all. O Jesus of Nazareth, through miracles of grace whose number is known but to Almighty God, I am your very little sister. I give, I know not what, nor do I wish to know. This is enough. I give.

Wednesday, December 11

Thank you, precious Co-missionary of Jesus, for the letter today from Father Keith. You know I treasure each as a precious gem of his Love, yet desire not that he make the sacrifice it must cost to send me but one note. His co-missionary I shall be forever, not by adoption nor appointment, but through the kindness of a Mother's love. God only knows how I can never be another Gertrude, a brilliant Red Rose such as she. Even as a little nothing have I failed him. Yet the joyous but painful fact remains that you have asked that I prolong your life lived entirely for Jesus. And by some miracle of Divine Love I remain here for him. This is all; it is enough. And it IS incomparable with any other's story, for it is ours alone. To compare is to cease to understand. Confidently, simply, I accept.

I seem to see Father Keith's face more and more, yet I desire to be with him less and less. I wish only to be to him what you were to Jesus, no more, no less. I wish to be jostled in the multitudes. If only I may serve with my nothingness, I wish nothing more. Even the thought of eternal union with him in Jesus is secondary. This joyous helplessness seems almost a goal itself. Thus my time with him is becoming almost burdensome, for I am not what I long to be for him. This I give. Please, O please make him yet more like Jesus.

Monday, December 16

It was such fun this morning to take each tiny, hand-carved figure of the Nativity set Father Keith got me in Bethlehem, and to place it atop the festive decorations, that it may catch our eye with its simple reality and lead us far beyond tinsel to the world's fairy tale: THE WORD IS MADE FLESH.

For the rest of the day all I've done is to sign my name — nearly 200 times. How awkward, and joyous. Little Virginia of Jesus. Isn't it beautiful? When it was first traced upon my heart, branded there with the heat of Divine Love, I was afraid to let others know. It seemed so irreverent that I, His poor little nothing, should bear His name. I know I am not worthy; my loved ones know, too. Perhaps I was afraid they'd *tell* me so. But now what difference would that make? If they recognize this, they've recognized Truth; and Jesus is the Truth. To see my unworthiness is to discover Jesus. Then nothing matters. For eyes will never more focus on anything else, not myself, not anyone, but forever will they seek this Face Whose brilliance is blinding, and they will bless the darkness.

Tuesday, December 17

Father wasn't able to offer Holy Mass for us today. Mother, will this be taken from us again? Even the security of these spiritual refreshments is taken, that venturing out into the dark night of Faith; we are at last free from all anxieties, even those concerning gifts that apparently bring such riches to our poor souls. I understand not what Our Father has in store, nor how He will bestow His Love upon me. Nor must I desire to understand. Just lead me Home, to Jesus.

This evening, after the others had left chapel, Sister Ann Joseph helped me to prepare a crib for your precious Baby, just as she once helped little second graders. O Mother, I have nothing lovely to put here for Him. It's all so cold and rough, all this within me, where precious Jesus will be laid. I'm sorry, Mother. How you must wish a nicer heart in which to give birth to your beautiful One. Please never forget how He loved poverty and lay Him here. You, His beautiful one, need but stay with Him here, and this tiny one will be content.

Friday, December 20

Daddy was here a while today, and he brought gifts, lovely gifts. I'm very pleased, Mother dear, for I can't remember the last time he could afford a Christmas present for me. This means so much, that he has given me something, for a special day. That he remembered what I'd written on my little Christmas list. Do tell him I'm very happy, and we needn't say why, do we? Somehow this little time with him has meant more than any other Christmas with him. May Jesus bring to him, too, this joyous peace that permeates my thoughts of him tonight, my Daddy.

What delight that electric vigil light brings he could never know. Its warmth, companionship, and red glow that enflames all who dare approach are constant reminders of the Sacred Heart of Jesus, longing to assure me that never need I be lonely; and a symbol of the poverty I troth to Him for all Eternity. That little bulb may burn out, but this little heart must burn on until it can no longer be distinguished from the Flame of Divine Love which consumes it.

Jean graced our home with her presence once more this evening. As we listened to the narrative of "The Littlest Angel," she trimmed my hair. We also rearranged our corner so that I might have my new vigil light near the only outlet. It looks so sweet, this, Baby Jesus' corner. Now it's time for rest, and when I turn out this little lamp, the room will be bathed in that red glow and peaceful happiness. Then, with the dawn rejoicing, as the Sun of God comes forth.

Father Keith, Father Jim O'Neill,
and Virginia share a lighter moment

five
❦

DECEMBER 23, 1963, TO MARCH 22, 1964

During the months covered in this volume, Virginia speaks of growing fatigue and chronic pain. The situation at "Good Sam" continues to deteriorate. Imperceptibly, at first, Virginia is being led into the Dark Night. More and more frequently there are references to inner desolation and emptiness. She writes: "I rejoice that Jesus is at last leading me to the sweet silence He's wished to share with me for so long. O how I thank Him for all the lessons He's taught me recently. Illness is but a retreat in which we may learn that which alone we need to learn, Jesus Christ and Him crucified." As she prepares for Easter, 1964, she writes: "The flesh is so tired, my throbbing head, my fumbling hands. But my soul longs to watch with Him Who is in such anguish and loneliness, fright and joyous resignation. Father, glorify your little girl that her whole life become a living Gospel of Jesus' Love!"

+

LOVE

Monday, December 23, 1963

It's soo late, and I've yet to do wrapping, Christmas cards, or packing amid this impenetrable quiet longing that fills my poor heart. Please come, Little One. Good night, sweet Mother. I know not when I'll get to visit with you like this again. And I'll miss it, somehow. But now I rush to Bethlehem to hear what angels have sung in the silent murmurings of your Immaculate Heart. May this always be the only sound your little ones hear when they enter the lovely stable of Jesus' eternal Birth.

Sunday, January 5, 1964

O Mother of Jesus, I offer tonight the terrible futility of words. It's an effort to type, to think. I'm but a baby, newly born, yet I presume to undertake a visit with you, who ponders the silence of Jesus' birth in your heart? Forgive, O please forgive. May I hide the ugliness of all this beneath your mantle? Like the Littlest Angel, I sob because I see that beside others', mine to give is ugly, irreverent, and even before I've begun this letter I almost wish to reclaim it, push it back into oblivion that my own gnawing sinfulness be not seen. But it seems too late. The whisper of almighty God has sung upon my lowliness. "These contents are of the earth, and of men, and My Son was born to be King of both. These are the things He, too, will love and cherish and then, regretfully, will leave behind." So I now begin to tell you that which is stored for all Eternity in the wordless realm of Love and offer my incessant failure. May it be lost in the poverty and darkness of the cave in which Almighty God left your womb to be cradled in your arms and BEHOLD YOUR FACE.

A full two weeks have passed, as earthly time is told. But to the eternal Now of God in which you reign Queen, these are the "Weeks that Are." I was O so happy to be in Nazareth [*the Tanzillis*] again, where for a little while I may speak often to Jesus, and most of all where I may listen to Him. But it makes little difference where He leads His little hobo anymore. Knowing that He is everywhere is enough. It wasn't hard to leave that little Nazareth Wednesday. Though I know not when I might return, still I didn't feel a door slam behind me. Thank God! Please offer it to your Baby, these spots in which there is always room for Him and His, to which a hobo might come and "Go in Peace."

Friday, January 10

Yes, beautiful Mother, it's time to rest once more, to fling myself into your embrace so that you can offer me to Jesus. Beauteous prelude to the hour of our death, when at last we shall awake to sleep no more. O to behold the Face of Christ in its entirety, and yet live because I peek through your mantle.

Mother dear, what is this ache? It just won't go away. Mostly in my legs, nothing sharp, just this dull monotony of hurt for days. It permeates all my waking hours, somehow fostering Divine Romance. Yet a feeble reminder of the soul aching for her God.

Sunday, January 12

O painful nothingness that I thank Our Father for tonight. I couldn't remain alert, yet sleep wouldn't come; my back begged me to kneel on the floor, but the incessant ache in my legs told me to remain in the chair; my body begged for the relief of sleep, but my soul magnified the Lord. This I offer tonight, and the joy of knowing I have a missionary so in love with Jesus.

Monday, January 13

Today, Holy Mother Church brings to life for us the Baptism of Jesus, and the magnificent manifestation of the Blessed Trinity Itself to mortals such as we here this evening. Mother, please teach me of Jesus that I might imitate Him, that I might prolong His very Life each minute of the day and night because He dwells within me. Help me to thank Him for the precious gift of Baptism. Often I forget, but lovely Mother, I'm sure that you remember. Let no prayer of mine ever reach Him but that has first passed the sweet portals of your Immaculate Heart.

Tuesday, January 14

Good evening, dear Queen of my little corner. How lovely you look atop the chest of drawers, above all else reigning sweetly, receiving my all that you may refashion it for Jesus. Yes, I left your image beside Little Jesus' on the paten. I just couldn't bear to put it away with the other tiny carvings. I love you so, Mother. You know how truly ugly that tiny carving is. Never have I seen your face so marred, and there is no other image of you I love more. Always the world shows you above the clouds, clothed in gold, so far, so very far away. They seem so insistent upon portraying your beauty. Please forgive my disappointment each time I see your picture or a statue representing you. They seem to say, "Don't touch Mother's dress; your hands are dirty." But no, they cannot keep me from you. I'm too little. I should die without you. So I scramble another way, darker, steeper, yet all the while your Immaculate Heart sings to me; and here is your embrace. O Mother, take me to Jesus.

Thursday, January 16

It was strange waking up this morning. My desk light was burning. I was completely dressed, shoes, my good suit. Various articles lay scattered on the floor. It was a strange feeling, everything topsy-turvy, not knowing just where anything had been placed. But even then I was conscious of its value. It's so convenient to awake each morning, clothing laid out, a definite schedule by which to wash, dress, no interferences. There's such a sense of security in it all. But now and then to have everything taken, knocked out from under one's feet, will surely teach us the stupidity of independence and how we little children are truly completely dependent upon Divine Providence for each lovely second of our existence. Please thank Our Father for this stunning reminder, and help me not to forget.

Friday, January 17

My beautiful angel was most kind to awaken me at three this morning. Once more I'd become too tired to prepare for bed so found myself completely dressed. I scrambled into my nightie, then kept watch for a little while before dawn Friday morning. It was God's day; it was "good." Where were you when your Jesus was prisoner that dark, dark night? Your body must have kept watch, your heart must have raced, throbbing, to be with Him, your soul crushed under the reality of your impotence, while every piece of Jesus' humanity called to you in Pain. O deep red rose, Jesus crushed you that your beauty might be preserved for all eternity. He loved you too much to gently hold you and watch your petals fall and wither. Tell Him I await Him, His burden, and if it should crush me, I shall magnify Him.

Saturday, January 18

Please, beautiful Queen of heaven and earth, help me once more crush the hateful designs of the Old Boy. He keeps suggesting comforts to me. I must push him back. Sometimes he sounds almost reasonable, but Faith is in heights that reason will never attain.

I suffer so poorly. I forget His Sacred Presence so often. Please beg His forgiveness. I want to love Him. I'm so glad there is something He permits me to return to Him. But I become so restless. I long to run to the phone to hear a dear one's voice. All day I fought this, but tonight I succumbed. I called Jean. How lovely her voice. Why could I not hear Jesus' all day? Wrapped in this shell of self-pity I forgot all else but discomfort. How many miracles did I not see today because I didn't take time to turn away from self? I know not. But if His mercy should give me yet another day, please open my eyes wide to see Him everywhere, my ears to hear Him knock, my heart to welcome Him that He may consume my entire being. Passion of Christ, make me your motionless altar.

Sunday, January 19

All day I read and listened to music and tried to sing and pretended to sleep. Why did I pretend, here in this little corner alone with Jesus? Not to foolishly try to deceive Him, but myself. Perhaps if I'm convinced I've rested, though I've but tossed, I can forget discomfort and keep on. You see, Mother dear, I've not yet learned to BECOME what He wishes, when He wishes. Please patiently continue the lessons. I don't wish to stop; I'm just weary, just a beginner, and, O splendorous hope, you're my Mother, and Jesus'.

Friday, January 24

It is good to have the weight of my uselessness always as the sands of the desert burying my heart. The seed must die, the death seems so slow and painful, but its memory will cease when the splendorous blossom of Jesus' Love appears.

Monday, January 27

I've hurt Jesus once more? I know, how painfully I know. The precious burden He's designed just for me I've distributed to others. Yet it becomes more intolerable. I complain of God's gifts. I tell my brothers and sisters, you, even the loving Giver of all gifts how heavy they are. Yet He must have wished to give so much more, if only I would bear it. *Accipio*. With great joy I accept. Please tell Him so. O joyful combat! Love, please give me no rest until there is no more of me left in Your consuming Flame. Live, Love, in a priest for whom your handmaid burns.

Now I go to lie beneath that soft light that says God is here. This little corner is such a sweet chapel for Him. My eyes will soon close; my mind slips beyond my power. Yet my heart will throb and my chest rise and fall, my body a temple moved by the Presence of its Creator. Come, Mother, please stay with me. Let us adore.

Wednesday, January 29

Days are long, very long, for little nothings. The only time I've used Anita is for this letter to you. I sleep much, but still awake to this ache, and worse, this listlessness. I'm tired; thank God I'm too tired to be anything but His little nothing. If I am Jesus', then surely He is mine, His prayer is mine too, for I cannot pray. With nostalgic pleading, I can but call out for Our Father.

Your precious Ruthie [*Zimmerer*] came for a little while this evening. It was as if the sunrise came at 8 p.m. There was her smile, and your Son, Who apparently forgot us today, walked into this corner, into my heart. O please give Him a thousand welcomes. Adore Him here. Press Him, and His Holy Cross, into depths of my heart I have not yet discovered, that its beatings be but echoes of true Love. Let us adore.

Thursday, January 30

Now is the wonderful time with you. How I anticipate these precious moments all day long, to gaze once more into your face and listen to the songs of your heart. Mother, you are so beautiful. Thank you for always being here, waiting for me to stop my play to come to you.

Sometimes I can't imagine having anything else to offer Jesus, Who is Himself the Father's Gift. But surely He can find sweet nothings He's lavished upon me continually and pretend that these are "mine to give."

In this recent helplessness, I've discovered just how tiny He is, how easy to cuddle close when all else seems too heavy and exhausting. I do not embrace the Cross; I'm being nailed to it. Rather, upon my heart rests One, tiny almost beyond perception. He isn't heavy; He's sweet and soothing and all else seems to fade into oblivion. I'm not suffering, only holding a Little One, Him, the Least.

Sunday, February 23

Mother, my beautiful Mother, now happily I fling myself into your arms, exhausted, filled with some unknown strength, joyous. It's been long since my last note to you, yet we remain together always, and I seem to forget just how long it's been, or even that any time has lapsed. It is always in the eternal Presence of God. We but seek and we do find, just as Jesus promises, for God's kingdom has come. WE are His kingdom. My soul trembles. But it remembers that you are here and there is Peace.

Blessed be God for this holy season. Somewhere in my throat is a cry, "My God, my God, why hast Thou forsaken me?" It just stays there. It's an ache. But there are no tears, no sound. This desolation is for Jesus alone to hear, while others sleep. I watch with Him so poorly. Perhaps this desolation of my waking hours will soothe His distress. Talking, even for this noisy little sister, is becoming a chore. I'm tired. And I rejoice that Jesus is at last leading me to the sweet silence He's wished to share with me for so long. O how I thank Him for all the lessons He's taught recently. Illness is but a retreat in which we may learn that which alone we need to learn, Jesus Christ and Him crucified.

Thursday, February 27

No Jean or Mary or Lou this morning with whom I might at last speak of Jesus' Love, so obvious yet sometimes so subtle within me. And this evening I waited long, filled with hope of seeing Ruthie's beautiful face, but Jesus seemed to ask that I stare at the night instead and be filled with the hope of beholding His Face soon. This exile is dark, and all "good" planning is brought to stupidity in the smile of Divine Providence. Silly little children magnify their Father's Wisdom, don't they? I don't want to be ashamed of that which pleases Him. Rather, I am delighted in His delights. O boundless Love that would keep such ugly poverty in existence, AND LOVE IT.

As I flung myself at Jesus' feet today in what is becoming a period of fatigue and ache, Sister Raphael came in to tell me that she was moving me once more from my corner. It is good to be recognized for the little hobo that I am, to be asked to step down because another more deserving of my room is coming. With the tired joy of a pilgrim I once more packed my knapsack.

And here we are, Mother, in a sweet new shrine. No one can guess what a move costs, and that's fine. Sister doesn't realize the multitude of adaptations a handicapper must make with each new surrounding, nor the mental work needed to draw them up. The room is hardly two-thirds as big as our last one, and maneuvering this little VW here is such a challenge. There are only certain spots where I can turn, one where I can make a complete circle. The terrazzo floor isn't quite so inviting, and the cold will be, thank God, my companion till winter is past. But then in the summer there will be the breezes dancing. And already sunshine streams in the windows to adorn everything with gold.

Saturday, February 29

O Mother, the beautiful discovery Jesus reserved for this Mary little Saturday. Suddenly I ceased the letter I'd been typing. All ceased but Love. The amazing realization that I sit, right here, this very moment, directly above the Tabernacle of our Beloved is thrilling beyond words. The thought makes me wish to be on the floor. It will never seem so cold, so hard now that His Eucharistic Presence cushions my days and nights. What Little Sister could desire any other Fraternity than this Our Father has kindly fashioned? Last night, after I'd written to you, I shifted a few things, and now the room looks twice as big and so nice. The sweetest room in our house, and O how God knows my unworthiness. In poverty is He magnified.

Wednesday March 4

It's been a cloudy, drizzly day, one just right for a little hobo to nap. Just nestled here so close to Jesus, in Our Father's arms, once more delighting in the knowledge that He loves His little nothing.

Our dear Maudey sleeps there forever now, in His peaceful embrace. She left our exile about 3:30 this afternoon. When I see my brothers and sisters go Home I am so filled with joy. No more will they suffer nor be crushed in the press of loneliness. And Christ Glorified becomes yet more entire. How sweet that I should hobo this way just before Maudey was called Home, that each time I left my sweet corner there she was. I held her hand; she kissed mine. That was enough. She'd grown too weak for talk. That little pilgrim was surely traveling lightly. All of her possessions that had to be gathered were her teeth, her glasses and one photograph. And now All is hers. Alleluia! If ever that word was significant, it's at the death of a Christian.

Thursday, March 5

Faith. Please beg that mine be strengthened, Mother. You know my needs well. How many times each day do we sinners call upon our Mother's prayer to obtain for us God's mercy? O for a faith which wouldn't bring tears to Jesus' eyes because it is yet so insufficient, a living faith that will remind Him of yours, Mother, and please Him. One that will move the hearts of men to Him, a far greater feat than the moving of mountains.

Monday, March 9

Poor old "Ellie Vator" wasn't able to serve this morning. Cold weather is mighty rough on what ails her. So I got to greet Jesus in THIS tiny chapel. I was kneeling on the floor. It's hard and cold, but He's so near this spot I don't notice anything else much. During Lauds I looked out to see the sky becoming more and more golden. How glorious God's visible creation. Who can imagine the designs of Divine Grace, or the Heart of a Mother filled with all that is God? But I'm your child, and in my silly fancies I'll continue to try.

Tuesday, March 10

This evening please take my poor little offering for my missionary. Make it lovely because you've merely smiled upon its lowliness. Here it is, Mother, all the anticipation of being with him again today and the emptiness and the waiting that filled this day when the weather didn't permit me the joy of his presence; that my heart might experience once again the yet deeper joy that time and distance between us weave. Somewhere out there in that night he goes about his Father's business and ours.

Wednesday, March 11

Somehow, today brought "Charlie's" "All my plans turn out to be mere bits of paper" from a new depth of my being. Futility is so painful, yet what can lead us more quickly to seek the Omnipotence of Our Father?

Thursday, March 12

Dawn's break brought us a thrilling view of God's winter wonderland. Everything was fairyland sparkle and innocent purity. Thank God for eyes with which to behold such, and for a heart that knows a seed lies dreaming happy things beneath its fluffy blanket.

Monday, March 16

Like the statues in our chapel, Jesus' presence in some souls is cloaked and hidden from the human heart. [*Formerly, statues in Catholic churches were covered over for a time during Lent.*] Though I am sometimes blind before these living tabernacles, I truly believe that He is there. Please consume your little one's feeble faith in your own simple protestation of Truth, "Here I am, God's little servant girl."

Wednesday, March 18

Mother, I've been a very poor Little Sister this Lent, you know. My arms are empty. I, the silly little hobo who used to delight in bringing little gifts you might offer Jesus: cold water in the morning, lack of blankets at night, all kinds of little goodies with which I might satisfy MY need to give to my Love. And now? Yes, Mother, my arms, my heart are so empty. And there is nothing to fill them but Jesus. Anything else is painful defeat. I am but desire. Only to know Jesus Christ and Him crucified is enough, and anything else would but mock this hunger.

Saturday, March 21

Two years ago today, there was a day of recollection and Love calling to Love, and a little Nazareth for a hobo's very own. Just for a little while. It was lovely. [*Virginia is referring to meeting Velma Tanzilli for the first time.*] Today I can return to its remembrance with a hobo's freedom and, without turning back, relive it and weep and find that I possess nothing but that unbearably selfish ache. Because I've grown weary of clutching it to my heart, at last I can SEE Nazareth. It's lovely; at last, it's mine. But it's gone, and we're on our way to Jerusalem with Jesus. I know, and with all pilgrims I go this Way with a song in my heart, a tiny *Magnificat.*

Sunday, March 22

Holy Mother Church helped us to gather our palms this morning and joyously throng to greet our King. But then, as She read the Holy Gospel to us, those palms withered and became distorted, and our hands seemed to hold knotted cords, a bush of thorny branches nearby. My soul, already in anguish, plunges into this week so appropriately called holy. Please let me remain with you each second, and may as much of your anguish my soul is capable of bearing be poured upon my trembling spirit. The flesh is so tired, my throbbing head, my fumbling hands. But my soul longs to watch with Him Who is in such anguish and loneliness, fright and joyous resignation. Father, glorify your little girl that her whole life become a living Gospel of Jesus' Love!

Virginia, circa 1965

six

~~~

APRIL 3, 1964, TO SEPTEMBER 6, 1964

*V*irginia begins volume six with an account of her third visit to
St. Meinrad's during Holy Week, 1964. The unofficial Kokomo
Jesus-Caritas Fraternity makes great strides; a tremendous spirit of
love pervades their small group. They make a weekend retreat at St.
Meinrad's. Virginia renews her vows privately on August 15th at
the Motherhouse chapel in Tipton, during the ceremony at which
several young ladies take public vows as new members of the religious community there. Virginia is plunged deeper into the Dark
Night of the Soul. She writes: "Prayers, sweet aspirations that have
filled my days since early childhood, O Mother, they're fleeing from
me. Your rosary, the Stations of the Cross, where are they? All is consumed in the Gospel, in the living Gospel to which we add a page
each day. But why do I still turn back to look for these consolations
that are behind? Look up, my soul, into this blinding light. Someday
you'll behold the Face of Christ." The volume concludes with
Virginia's preparations to participate in a pilgrimage to Marian
shrines in Canada.*

+

LOVE

[After spending Holy Week at St. Meinrad's]

Rejoice and be glad, beautiful Mother, Alleluia, for Jesus lives in our glorified weakness! Joyously have I anticipated this little time with you. O to see your face, to feel your embrace, to know that you have embraced your glorified Son and see the joy of it vibrate through your entire being. Mother, you are beautiful! Your face, your hands, your heartbeat, these are curtained from our blindness, our distorted vision that would but mar your features with our own ugliness. But your being, pulsing with joyous adoration of the Supreme Being Whose great delight is to be yours, somehow vibrates your affections through the poor little one who leans heavily and always upon you. What wordless *Magnificat* fills my being!

And in my riot of joy I try to put a bit of it on paper. Please beg forgiveness for this futile attempt. All my actions are thus, condemned to uselessness and worse. But the Holy Church that tells us Jesus was crucified, died, and was buried in the same breath triumphantly proclaims that her glorious Spouse rose from the grave to reign forever and ever in His Father's Kingdom. That is hope; that is why I come to you. "No, not I. . ."

ST. MEINRAD'S! Mother, is it that you've given your poor little hobo another "special spot" at last? It's nice to keep going Home and in my heart have an idea of that which "eye hath not seen nor ear heard nor hath it entered the heart of man." Joyous part, these memories that will never be taken from us, but will nourish our weakness until there will no longer be memories or anticipation. Surely no little sister was welcomed and loved as I, for those men become gentle and stoop to serve the Christ that reflects from their eyes in my wheels.

Now I must rest. Thank you, O thank you, beautiful Mother, for All. I am so tired; but two or three hours was all the rest I could get each night. But now I have my big chair again and perhaps a little, just a little, comfort and rest that the strength to accomplish Our Father's Will be mine, no more, no less. Once again Jesus dwells beneath me. So close, so wonderful! Please adore Him, Mother, for us.

Sunday, April 12

Sleep won't come, Mother. But you are here, and Jesus, and restlessness becomes blessed. I love you, and Jesus, and "Sam." I'm weary and filled with joy that in but four hours it will be time to rise and greet the day the Lord has made and rejoice and be glad in it. O Night, so dark and long and sweet and silent and God-clad, you are beautiful. I know this pecking disturbs none of my dear family here. Only Jesus, immediately beneath Anita, can hear. Will He be pleased to help me write to you, Our Mother, as We keep watch together? Surely He will.

Mother, I wish I could be more like you. Though your heart was heavy, I know you didn't bother Jesus to lift the weight from you. Queen of co-missionaries, I am yet so unlike you, so unworthy to even wish to continue your work. But I give my all to you and beg that you make it a worthy gift. It's been a hard week, Mother. Please find a note of gratitude in my complaint. Such a spoiled little girl am I. And now, for weeks, for months, Our Father hasn't delighted me with all the little goodies He used to send. Yet the sweetness of this frightful darkness is as no other gift He has sent, and I love it as I could love no other. Its bitterness is untold sweetness.

At last to Holy Mass this morning. Mother, the entire week seemed to rest upon this hope: Holy Mass. All else seemed to have been taken, everything but the consolation that once again I could approach the altar of God and be replenished with His joy. But now I see that I was bargaining with Love. Please beg forgiveness for me. Help me desire only my Beloved's happiness. Otherwise, I shall know only misery and shall be unworthy to be called a Christian.

Monday, April 13

All life is filled with sweetness can we but search beneath the surface. And who but this hobo could look in a pair of bobby socks and find joy? For in each pair Jean placed a greeting. I looked for all of them, for it was such fun. And here is the little stack of happiness. I offer it to you, Mother, for it's so lovely and I know it will delight your heart. To please her Mother is a little one's happiness.

Wednesday, April 15

Good evening, my beautiful Mother. All day I've been here pecking, trying so hard to put a dent in my correspondence pileup. And now I come to the most delightful time of all, a few words to you, and my mind is blank. I'm sorry. Still, it is a sweet goodnight because you are my Mother and your loveliness soothes my heart and you lay me to rest on the bosom of the Father. O that nothing take this from me!

Friday, April 17

My sweet Mother, did you love less I would expect you to scold instead of smile at my approach. Your arms are always waiting to enfold me. O blessed assurance.

Your silly little one just awoke, and here it is only 11 p.m. I came up early from this evening's visit with Jesus; was just too exhausted for anything but sitting in that comfy chair. Now here I am, nearly five hours later, feeling that the day should be beginning. Yet it is dark and silent and night will not lift for so long a time. And with the dawn, rejoicing. Now I wait in peace, for Jesus is near, so very near, in the chapel below me, but also, miracles of Love, within my poverty He delights to remain. Please come, let us adore Him.

Monday, April 20

Always you're here, and there is nothing in which you're not interested. I know, Mother, for somehow, by some condescension of Infinite Mercy, I hear often the sweet murmurs of your tender, Immaculate Heart. You seem to invite me to share everything with you. Others haven't time to listen to my silliness. No, I can't blame them. They speak of responsibilities and rather frown upon me because they think I know nothing of these. But you await me! O Mother, I wish I could be a pretty little girl, one you might be proud of. But most of all I wish to be forever your child, and in this is contentment. Will you not teach me those things that please you most? Then shall I remind you of Jesus and find you smiling upon me.

Thursday, April 23

Big, wonderful Gus [*St. Augustine*] told me today, "The Christian spirit must be renewed by frequent watchings through the night." Yes, Mother, it is late, and it is Thursday night. "Can you not watch one hour?" the lonely Lover pleads. What heartless little sister could even think of fatigue and pain? My desires are so great, but I so small.

Sunday, April 26

Lovely, understanding Mother, you can see that I am so weary as I approach you this evening. The Old Boy tells me to wait till tomorrow for our visit. But no, your sweet goodnight is too precious. Joyfully I find you here and forget that I am weary in the enthusiastic homecoming of your caress.

Wednesday, April 29

After our "Charlie" meeting this morning, Mary Romack and I stopped for a cherry milkshake. It's such fun trying to get the crazy cherries through the straw, blowing them out and sucking and dribbling, straw after straw breaking under the pressure. All life is fun and funny and wonderful in the eternal Presence of God. If He stays not with us, life is death. But He promised, "I am with you always." I believe. Please, Mother, help my unbelief and let my heart be lost in the adoration you pour before Him.

Thursday, April 30

Wasn't sure which date to use, Mother. It's really Friday, May 1st, 2 a.m. I love you and joyously welcome this month entirely dedicated to you. A thought of you is joy; a month of you irrepressible delight. So my little heart will consider but each day, or burst.

Wednesday, May 6

What O what for my missionary tonight? In shame I come to the conclusion of this day. Perhaps I might offer for him the heat that has all kinds of things going on under my "halo" [*neck brace*]? That's not such a nice gift, is it? Then what? Nothing! Yes, this I give. It makes you smile so slightly, and surely that can be the sunshine that will bless his weary path tomorrow. Now to rest upon this happy thought. We love you, Mother, I and another so like Jesus. I'm so tired tonight. Hardly know what I'm telling you. But that makes no difference. You always understand, whether I come babbling with excitement or heavy with fatigue. Please stay with me. Good night, Mother.

Friday, May 8

Will I ever keep watch worthily? My flesh, even my spirit, is woefully weak. When I awoke this morning, there I was kneeling completely dressed, again. And Jesus, waiting, alone. Does He love my wishes? That's all I have, and even they are puny. But here. Please make them lovely, for Jesus. You know what He loves most. Tell Him I love being His silly little nothing. Someday I hope that my wishes will be absorbed in His and the Father will be well pleased.

Sunday, May 10 [Virginia's twenty-second birthday]

Good evening, Mother. The night is sweet and still, with fragments of today's festive remembrances strewn about. It is late and I am tired, and if ever my "Our Fathers" would be mixed up with my "Hail Marys," it would be tonight. But my prayer is not so lovely. I just peck and peck and wonder how my heavy eyes and fumbling fingers can ever tell you what my heart says. A little one takes a pencil into his hands and finds a scrap of paper and delightfully begins scratching. After all, when grown-ups write it just looks like so many nonsensical curlicues. And often they seem more reluctant to explain than the little one. He eagerly reads his "love ya's," wondering at the grown-up's lack of comprehension. But Mother, she always knows. HAPPY MOTHER'S DAY! It is a joyous day because Jesus loves you so. Me too.

Wednesday, May 13

The little brother to whom you've given my heart called this morning and asked if we might take a trip to the clinic today. Our day together was heaven-sent, but really, Mother, I sympathized with that doctor. Is he that personally concerned with each patient? He just said, "O Ginny, Ginny, Ginny!" when he saw my spasms, that the Soma [*medicine*] is no longer effective. So now I must stop all medication till Friday noon, at which time I begin a more potent drug. O Mother, will it help? And what of all day tomorrow? Even now my head is throbbing. I'll lay low so as not to disturb anyone and rejoice that there is a little gift for my missionary.

I've got to scoot now, Mother dear. Please fling me in all confidence and hope into the bosom of the Father to rest. My nothingness will be His delight, His glory, and His smile my eternal bliss.

Thursday, May 14

Hi Mother, it is your little spasm here to delight in being with you, in knowing that she is yours, that you can truly love her in your maternal caress so great it contains a universe and all Heaven itself.

Friday, May 15

Mother dear, Norma just awoke me to get ready for bed. Surely the medication won't prevent my writing tonight's "love ya." Just to find you here, then to fall asleep once more in your arms, is so sweet. You know how long my poor body has needed this rest. Please let it be an act of abandonment, in which you place me in the strong arms of Our Father. I love.

Saturday, May 16

Mother, your little dishrag comes once again in a heap of poverty at your feet. I almost wish to ask forgiveness for loving you so much. I'm so ugly. Just use me to wipe off the stains that make souls less pleasing to Our Father. Though I myself am yellowed, being yours will make Him forget my sinfulness.

Jesus and His Father look upon little ones gathered in prayer with their Mother. Because They delight to find your loveliness among us, They hasten to send the Spirit of Their Love to transform us. And you will be happy to look at us and find Jesus with you again. O to see you smile!

Wednesday, May 20

Mother, all is so heavy this evening. Every little task demanding almost more than I have to give. Every decision frightening. Every idle word that pours from me a humiliation. Thinking itself is work, and speaking, and moving. I am so weary. And the new medication simply pronounces this fatigue. To think that I am chosen to reveal the splendors of Jesus' Love to these little ones is too much. I see myself, miserable, and I sob. O how I long to possess and be possessed by Jesus' Love. I give you — desires.

Sunday, May 31

Good evening, lovely queen of all Hearts. Once again it's so late, I know, yet I just can't resist the joy of a visit with you. How I've yearned for the moments, perhaps hours, we spend here together and then those during which you take me to gaze into the Mystery that is your Son and to find the Light not blinding because your sweetness reminds Him how weak are little ones. Please remind my lonely heart of Jesus. Surely if it but thinks of Him it will be satisfied. Tell Him I'm sorry for being so forgetful. How filled have these days been, filled with suffering and Glory. Please let me learn how synonymous these are.

Mother, how joyously I bring something of beauty for you — this letter from Father Eugene. Please tell him what a consolation it is to find him always with me in the shadow of the Cross. So often we silly children begin to hide our pains, secretly pleased with the daily martyrdoms we feel we offer Jesus. But then there comes one to whom we give our love and with it all else. All walls are shattered, all those defenses in which we took such secretly selfish pleasure. Stripped and ugly and shivering from our own coldness, we are warmed by the embrace of one who loves far above and beyond all that we are or are not. Mother, it is sweet. Thank you for sending Jesus thus. It's nice to be "tough," but never do I wish to forget that I am your little one.

Sunday, June 7

Blessed be God in this day He made for His little ones! It was so nice. I listened to that tape Anne-Marie recorded for me a couple years ago. It's completely dedicated to Childlike Simplicity and filled with reminders of little Jesus, His Little Flower, all the mysteries concerned in the Plan of a Father Who likes kids. Mother, how I treasure its message! I want to hear it again and again to begin to comprehend it. There is no other Way. The "wise" speak of maturity and independence. Please don't let them know the disaster of growing too big to be tossed into the Happiness of Our Father's bosom.

Monday, June 8

That Old Boy is pestering me again. Please Mother, smash him or something. I shan't give him this Peace I've at last found in serving as Our Father wishes. He keeps speaking of money and independence and responsibility, and he's tripped himself on the last issue. Heavy, so heavy is this responsibility. Having a missionary, trying to be a good little hobo belonging to no one but all; giving but never knowing the Gift, receiving always and receiving whatever one wishes to give me — in the love of your Child I accept this vocation and promise to cling to it lovingly because it is His.

Saturday, June 13

This afternoon my radio began smoking, and the fan Mary Cooperider brought me so kindly yesterday morning stopped. What with the lamp the wind blew on the floor last Wednesday plus the recorder that stopped recording for me night before last, it's getting funny, or something. O Mother, it's so good.

Tell Jesus to take all from me so that gleefully He can run with all His Littleness and Infinity into my heart. He is Everything; everything without Him despair.

Wednesday, June 17

Please take all that is mine to give, and ever more, Mother. I am very tired. Will you please help me prepare for the night? I feel so incapable; my head keeps falling upon my typewriter. Don't forget to give my poor gratitude to Our Father for making me so helpless today, and YOURS.

Thursday, June 18

Thank you, Mother dear, for getting me ready for bed last night, and for giving me such a long rest. It must have been nearly eight hours! You are kind. And I awoke to a strange dream. It seemed that little though my room was I had to have a roommate. It meant getting rid of almost everything. I grew panicky. "What about my letters, my prayer life, me?" But then the new bed, so white and waiting, caught my eye; CHRIST was moving in with me in another of His guises. However He chooses to come, I long to love Him with all that I am. Please thank Him for this sweet dream.

Sunday, June 21

Hello, Mother dear. Thank you for a big, wonderful, HILARIOUS weekend. Please take it this evening as an offering from my poverty to our Father on Fathers' Day. Usually we're told to offer to Him our pains, anguish, ugly selves. But it is sweet this evening to place in your queenly hands a whole weekend of laughter, of thorough enjoyment, of pure delight in the Divine Humor, in the beautiful thing called Truth, called Christ.

We just returned from Fátima Retreat House in Indianapolis a little bit ago. It was grand, and Father Charles Lees, what to say of him? How often must he broaden your smile as you hear him and remember that he, too, is your child. During our very first conference, Father said, "I hope you don't enjoy this retreat." O but Mother, we did, thoroughly. Why did we laugh so? Father was such a child, so tactless, so open, blunt, beautiful. And Jean shared this pleasure with me so thoroughly. We seemed to listen to each other's heart and delight to learn that we were singing together. It was wonderful, and though we broke silence incessantly, I can't feel Our Father was displeased that we looked upon His creatures and found them good and delighted in them together.

And there were lessons. Never is there a moment in which we may not learn more of a God named Divine Love. The first night was so blessed, and so dark. Sleepless, and happy to remain so, I sat there in His Presence, in the *terrible silence of God*. O how can my heart be so far from Him Who lives within it, in Whom it has its being? Let me be not foolish enough to wish to understand. I keep begging to have nothing but Him for my joy. Stripping is painful, and nakedness ugly, but this is easily forgotten, self-annihilated, before the brilliant countenance of God's eternal Thought, of Christ.

Saturday, June 27

Mother, I'm so glad you're here, always. Why this loneliness, forgetfulness? I've turned to the phone so many times today, but resisted. It's such a temptation. I cling so, yet all besides Jesus is terrible disappointment. I know. How I've awaited these precious moments with you this evening. You whisper of Jesus; there is nothing more, or less, to bring me comfort. Thank you.

It is still rather early. Perhaps I'll read a little, then kneel at your feet to watch you adore your Little One and rejoice that in my poverty I have no heart but yours with which to love Him. Please don't forget that this nagging ache in my legs is for a little brother whose Love brings good news of great joy to all.

Sunday, June 28

Thank you, Mother dear, for seeing that dear ones brought their little sister a fan this evening. Thank you also for the continued ache in my legs. Who am I to say which gift is more pleasing? I am entirely yours so that a priest becomes daily transformed into Christ. To be pleasing is all a little servant girl wishes.

Wednesday, July 1

A letter from your wee go-getter Ruthie Arreche, and quite the surprise. She tells me at last that she plans to have ME in her pilgrimage to your shrine in Canada come September. O Mother, please tell her of my loving gratitude. It has cost her much to make these wonderful plans for me.

Somehow pilgrimages hold no precedence in my desires. The Blessed Trinity has taken Its abode within my very ugliness. What shrine can lay a bolder claim? Yet simply BEING with poor little ones who give to their beautiful Mother their very helplessness will be my joyous privilege. My little wheels will be lost among so many; at last I shall hide, sore thumb that I usually appear. I can hardly wait to hide among those so in love with you, to be lost in their suffering and joy, to know it is enough that I am yours and you remember me.

Thursday, July 2

Please, Mother, loan your little slave your Immaculate Heart with which to magnify our God because He has looked with kindness upon my misery. Tell Him I gladly watch His sweet consolations flee; but never let me let Him go.

Tuesday, July 7

Mother dear, I bring today's mail to you this evening. I bring all, all nothingness. If you but love me I shall never feel shame in my poverty. Please let this little seed die, and blossom. Little ones are so hungry. Mother dear, I know I needn't say more. What little one can approach you without trailing the world?

Wednesday, July 15

Mother dear, these moments with you once again, how I love them. Your little hobo throws her poor self, her knapsack, her life and death passionately and peacefully into your arms. Enough babble. Now, Mother, hold me close, closer still, and tell me of Jesus.

Thursday, July 16

Mother, my Kokomo sisters grow lovelier each time I see their faces, hear their voices, feel their embraces; once again I bring my memories of them here for your sweet pleasure. How

Virginia auditioning for the Beatles?

can Jesus' Love be any deeper? Yes, Mother dear, I know we've hardly BEGUN. Happily your little children fall into this infinite chasm, together.

Wednesday, July 22 (Feast of St. Mary Magdalene)

Mother, I want to be a little one at His feet, watching, listening, resting there, refreshed. In the peaceful cloak that surrounds Us my eyelids may close. Still, in that darkness I'll hear His Voice, and if He should cease to speak I shall wait peacefully for another word and rest there, with Him. My dear ones call to me of responsibility, but He hushes them with speech of the best part, which He has chosen for me and which none can take from me, since the day I poured my all, tears and sweetness, upon His feet. He was pleased; others disgusted. But who can hear others' bitter remarks when His pitying eyes smile and He sends a sinner forth in peace? Weighty responsibility: "Sin no more."

Saturday, July 25

It will be a few days before I may write to you. I'll miss it; I do hope that the pleasures of these little visits aren't all mine. O how I wish to please you, Mother whom I love so.

Friday, July 31

Mother, I love you so! Thank you for being here and for loving me always. What the pain has been in my heart I do not know. This yearning for only One and the "apparent" possession of all but Him. Please, most faithful of all the wonders our Father has created, lead me far, far beyond the apparent to the realms of Faith and Love. I accept and love this darkness because it heralds the Light. I wait; please remove from me all desire to hasten the gifts for which Our Father is preparing me. "The Light shines in the darkness, and the darkness grasps It not." Please relish it, Mother, for one yet too little to be aware of the Heaven that is her heart.

Sunday, August 2

What has come over me? I know, yet I'm almost afraid to admit that I've been seized by Jesus. He lives! It's so that I can't tell if suffering or joy dominates, so intermingled are they within my poverty. He lives! A false humility accuses me for admitting this. But I cannot hide this gift. It is given in spite of my unworthiness, perhaps because of it, and that unworthiness isn't lessened by it. It's displayed yet more miserably in your Son's pure gaze. O Mother, please hear what words cannot say. Here's my heart, for Him.

Wednesday, August 5

My darling Sister Blanche was to have received the order's new habit today. May she be lovely and pleasing to the Bridegroom for Whom she wears her spotless garment. We thank you, Mother, earth-garment which alone was worthy to clothe our Creator. Please fashion these temples of flesh that He leap from Heaven to dwell within us because we remind Him of you.

Thursday, August 6

Somehow the miserable capacity of words to express what our hearts sing is staggering tonight. It is very late, Mother dear, and I almost fear the burden of fatigue is becoming my precious gift, to receive and to offer, once again. My strength seems to come and go, my preference for rest rather than the little duties on my daily schedule more pronounced. Thus far I've fought, and won. And if Jesus should somehow make me such a little nothing as He has in the past, I think it will be sweet just being His. "I am ready for all; I accept all." But right now please help me to abandon all thought of what my future capacities may be. I desire neither health nor sickness, but the Will of Him Who sent me, NOW.

Saturday, August 8

It's refreshingly cool tonight. Please take our rest that tomorrow we may give all to possess and be possessed by God.

Sunday, August 9

O Mother, Jesus' embrace is so warm and strong and relentless. Almost in spite of my cautious heart have you reassured me. The other night at Elwood, while I gave the answer to one of the discussion questions, I found my heart stuttering secretly of its own experience. And just as unknowingly, Father Keith told me that the suffering of which I spoke was that of the Dark Night of the Soul. O how I needed this assurance, and Jesus bid the winds to hush and returned to a little corner of my poverty to take His rest that at dawn We rise together in peace.

Monday, August 10

All is so costly. Please transform efforts into gifts.

Tuesday, August 11

This pecking must cease; Love is here.

Wednesday, August 12

Sweet little sister Pain was here all day. How welcomed is she, as she kisses my hip, my back and head, as she consecrates my heart.

Friday, August 14

Please teach us that the dawn's rejoicing follows our blindness. Thank God for this night in which tomorrow's dreams are formed. I dream I am at last pleasing to Jesus; because you're my Mother, I rest in confidence that this dream will be true.

Monday, August 17

Mother dear, it's just me, your little, tired hobo. There's so much bubbling in the poverty called my heart, but somehow weariness asks that it remain untyped and unsaid, here for Jesus alone. And I'm glad it's that way.

Saturday was beautiful, just as all Mother's Days, all days with you, in you, for you, through you, are. All my precious sisters from Kokomo were there at Tipton with me as his secret bride [*Virginia*] promised herself to Jesus once again. Those dewy drops on my cheeks were not the result of a little envy, as they might have been last year, but of overflowing joy in knowing that I am His and He is mine and all there is to anticipate is that soon I shall behold His Face. Meanwhile, I sit waiting at your feet. Please give this paper [*vows*] to our Father for me. You are lovely and He'll be pleased.

Thursday, August 27

O to watch and pray worthily but one hour with Jesus; to feel the guilt of the world gripping at me so vehemently that it saps me of all; to shudder in fear as with even greater joy the whisper vibrates through my entire being till it finds its voice and shouts in my heart, "Not my will but Thine be done!" Queen of the Winepress, don't forget that I'm yours.

Monday, August 31

How often have I crushed your Immaculate Heart during the past month? How often have I pleased you? Please never once forget me, inconstant that I am. Make me a good child.

In rushes September, big and laden with graces. Little ones everywhere return to school; me, too. I rush wherever His Voice calls to His little hobo. Let me run with no hesitation, with no consideration but that it is He Who calls Whose Love alone can fill my heart.

Thursday, September 3

Tonight Jesus let me come to speak with Him at last. Please thank Him for my heart that is hushed in remembrance of His words. "You suffer because your will is not My Will yet." Yes, I know. Please beg Him to purify me relentlessly till at last I may truly say that it is He Who lives within me.

It's very late and I must scoot, but this goodnight with you is so sweet, and it would be a shame to miss it for a half hour more given to my body's whims. This silly head; it's aching all over, so I must stop typing. Tell Him Who understands our weakness that I shall rise with Him soon for another blessed day of seeking the Will of Our Father and finding it in Him Who wants but that we ask.

Friday, September 4

This morning Jesus was exposed for us in the Blessed Sacrament, and the futility of prayer was at once heavy and blessed. Little ones sit listening at His feet. Why is this one so restless? Do teach her to sit still and wait and never forget to smile in His Presence. Somehow things He told me last night are returning to my poor memory. When little ones all around me were crying today, all noises seemed to blend into, "My God, My God, why have You forsaken Me?" Christ is saving the world; how could I NOT say *fiat* to this?

Sunday, September 6

I've been going in circles this evening packing, but things are resuming a little order. Jesus has much in store for His little hobo during this pilgrimage, I'm sure. Please help me to keep my heart wide open to receive gifts and to give. He speaks to me continually of penitence of late. I am so ashamed of my lack of voluntary sacrifice, unsought display of Love. Perhaps during these moments which will drain my bodily and spiritual poverty, I can begin to understand Jesus' longing for His Hour and His willingness to do anything to hasten it, to save the world, even my soul. How very many of my brothers and sisters cry out when I go to pray, when I stop to listen: a young boy awaiting a prison sentence, another alone and lost in a frightful world, a precious friend in cancer's painful clutches, "Sam," and all the anguish and cruelty that breed here, another fella searching, tired. It goes on and on, Mother. I hardly need mention my missionary. How wonderfully remembrances of him fill each moment of each day. For him, for the world, for the sake of the Gospel, I am a pilgrim and will remain so till I get Home. Even now Home is everywhere, because Home is God.

Virginia and friends

seven

⤙❦⤚

SEPTEMBER 14, 1964, TO APRIL 13, 1965

Book seven begins with a brief description of Virginia's Canadian pilgrimage. During the months covered in this book, Virginia visits St. Meinrad's twice. Despite her growing dissatisfaction with life at "Sam," she decides it is her vocation to remain there. Great changes in liturgical practices — such as the switch from Latin to English — initiated by the Second Vatican Council, creates division and confusion among Catholics. Virginia relates a few such experiences. She is plagued by aridity in her spiritual life. She writes: "Jesus appears to sleep. His Presence is so very subtle at times, but when I cry for Him He is saddened by my lack of faith in His Love, in His Living Presence within those around me. Only my love can reveal it to me. 'Lord, save us from ourselves!'"

+

LOVE

Monday, September 14, 1964

Mother dear, here I am alone at last with you. I'm so glad. Please take ALL from these recent days, purify it and toss it to lie forever in the oblivion of Our Father's glory.

This must be brief, for your little hobo has just hopped from Canada to New York to Indianapolis to Kokomo. But it must be, for I love you so. Thank you for welcoming me to your watchful heart always.

Cape de Madeleine, and Ste. Anne de Beaupré, they are good shrines, but somehow they seem no better than this evening in your arms chattering. I shall never have to travel thousands of miles, for Love has made my heart His abode. I do appreciate being with all those grand handicappers, grand Canadians, the whole grand bunch to whom I was introduced through this pilgrimage. "Merrily shall we meet in heaven."

It is time for a hobo to put her knapsack up and abandon all to Our Father for the night. Again, thank you, Mother.

Wednesday, September 16

Good evening, Mother. I've just returned from a day at Jean's. Here it is September and our gatherings are once more to be in my little sisters' homes. I've truly missed scooching in their corners. It's such joy to know we'll be sharing Jesus in this atmosphere once again. Long after I've gone, please let memories of the Love that was so visibly present as we gathered be visible still to these little sisters of Jesus, and to all with whom they come in contact.

Sunday, September 20

In this morning's lesson from the Holy Gospel, we watched the paralytic rise and carry his stretcher as a manifestation of the forgiveness of his sins by the loving Master. And also today you watched me try again to walk and fall into ever greater need of forgiveness. Mother, teach me to lie still, in complete resignation, to let myself be placed before your kind Son and know my sins are forgiven because you've spoken to Him of me and He can't refuse a Mother's faith in her silly little ones.

Thursday, September 24

This morning I phoned Father Keith about the most recent book of letters to you. It was wonderful to have a legitimate excuse to speak with him. Thank you, Mother. It was our privilege to have him read them during the pilgrimage, thus making our beautiful union yet more intimate as we prayed together for all the intentions that fill these pages. Last night I was trying to figure out how to get them back in time for our Meinrad trip this Saturday. Those letters seem such an integral part of my visits with Father Lucien. In his wisdom he reads and encourages and guides his little hobo sister through the painful poverty of her love for you and Jesus.

Friday, September 25

Please tell Our Father how His little hobo has appreciated this restful day. I can't remember ever having ALL correspondence cared for. It was sweet to be sitting at Jesus' feet all morning, the book in my hand simply an ornament for one too little for anything but listening.

Sunday, October 4 [After a visit to St. Meinrad's]

Beautiful, loving Mother of hobos, my mind seems lost in a maze of joy and anguish and my heart hushed in the Peace of Jesus Christ. What can I write to you tonight?

Words, words, words, please take them in reparation for my excessive speech. They come so painfully tonight. The perfectionist in me is inclined to resort to a void rather than the humiliation of not being able to express what fills my heart. I'll just let my fingers fumble these keys and hope that they find a way of expressing a fraction of what is in my heart. And in the disappointment of seeing that this is not possible, I will rejoice that you smile at the effort and incapacity of your little one.

I have loved Father Eugene but one year. It does seem forever and will be in the timeless haven for which we both pine. Please make Jesus' Love increase in our hearts daily. Right now I see not how I could share Love with any human more, but I would have said the same a year ago. What depths I hadn't dreamed of! How much greater will they become as I am tossed in all confidence and joy upon the boundless sea of Love? Together we remain beneath the Cross. Please let us stay here till "It is consummated" and death is our victory.

Here I am back at Sam once again, the strength of those days coursing through my heart. Thank you for the strengthening nourishment and rest. Now let me use them well for the pleasure and glory of Our Father. I return to Sam's antagonism and a mass of suffering humanity that is my heart, and with Jesus I "have come that they may have life, and have it more abundantly," because He has chosen to live in my poverty. Please let me not forget Him for an instant.

Tuesday, October 6

It is so sweet to remain lost in the security of your loving embrace, resting in the knowledge that you will see that your little hobo will wander where she can best resemble Jesus and thus bring you, her Mother, happiness as in your maternal solicitude you stoop to see to her needs. To see your smile will satisfy my every painful effort to be a good little one. I am anxious to know where this Little Way will lead; I follow, for somehow it will bring me closer to Home. Peace reigns because, "All the way to heaven is Heaven, for He said I am the Way." Home is the heart of my very being. How often little ones need to be reminded! Please continue your patience with me, Mother.

Wednesday, October 7

Queen of the Most Holy Rosary, in the chorus of praise that rises from the hearts of all your children today, I hide my own "love ya." Where are my beads? others may wonder. They haven't been seen tangled in my fingers for months. But you see my crystal garland of teardrops that winds about my heart to make it forever yours and Jesus'. Upon its salty beads are the words of the Holy Gospels. I do hope that you who have requested your children to say the Rosary daily are pleased with the poverty and love of my method.

Sunday, October 11

Mother of God — and please forgive the terrible contrast — my Mother, please accept the love note of a little sleepyhead on this feast of your Divine Maternity. Why this weariness; it's but nine o'clock? Please see that the soul and body of my missionary are refreshed as I scamper to the oblivion of your little nothings.

Monday, October 12

Daddy was here this afternoon. As we went out into the lovely fall day, we were met by a deaf-mute who gave us a card requesting alms. Thank God for sending him. As he walked away in his lonely little world I took quick stock. What can legs do for God or arms or a strong back compared to fingers that type and a tongue that echoes your *Magnificat*? I'm glad Father Eugene reminded me that even these could be taken. Take them now, my all, my nothingness, my sins and my virtues, my pulse, each breath. I am God's creature; He looks upon me and sees as only He can see that I am good, GOOD, like Him! Please let me never do anything to mar the image of Jesus, and Him crucified and triumphant, in me nor in anyone whom God sends to me to be warmed in His Love. In His beloved Son is He well pleased; please teach me to please Him as you do.

Wednesday, October 14

Mother, you know how often I've been asked to sing God's mercies in my life, and how often I've failed. [*Virginia is referring to the many requests she had received to write about her life.*] I want to sing; I do sing, but not as others would wish. "I shout the Gospel with my whole life," soar the hobo hopes within me. But all writing is hard but these letters to you. To know my nightly "love ya's" are pleasing to you and Jesus is enough. Should you ask that I discontinue them one of these days, still to die in your arms each night will be my goal.

Thursday, October 15

Ruth Arreche's card today brought the question, "Would you ever consider living in New York?" Mother, you know how often I've wished for this, yet try to rid myself of all wishes until I receive an indication of God's Holy Will for me. Is this it? To leave Nazareth that is yet so close yet gone forever for me, leave my precious little sisters here in Kokomo, go far from Hobo Haven [*St. Meinrad's*], which alone holds a semblance of home for me right now, to leave ALL and follow Christ and set all aflame with His Love as I go my Mary little way? How great my desires but never great enough.

Leaving Sam WOULD be painful, I'm sure. How strange that we should become attached to our sufferings. If this tangible poverty and all this anguish are taken from me, what will there be left? Nothing. Please help me to offer this greatest of gifts, devoid of all self-satisfaction, graciously.

Saturday, October 17

Strange that only this morning, in reading the summary of the life of St. Margaret Mary in our missal, did I discover the wonderful lesson my sister triumphant must wish to teach me: her girlhood marked by painful illness and even more painful family discord, her entrance to the convent at the grand age of 22, her ignorance, sickliness, clumsiness; but most of all Jesus' words to her, and me, for these please help me sing praise this evening. "I will make you so poor and vile and abject in your own eyes, and I shall destroy you so utterly in the thought of your own heart, that I shall be able to build Myself up in the void." Please, Mother, in the innocent audacity of a little one, I beg you to ask Jesus to let the Spirit of His Love do the same to me, that another stupid little creature somehow be a living reminder of Our Father's glory.

Sunday, October 18

Your restless, lonely little hobo comes to you with her good-night. I'm tired, Mother. It's time to once again press my tiny Jesus to my being, to learn of your meek and humble Son. Please help me. It's so hard to be a little nothing. Why is it hard, for it's been my prayer for so long? Only my deceptive feelings call for rebellion. But my heart goes on singing. *MAGNIFICAT.* . . .

Tuesday, October 20

Every moment Divine Love beckons to us. Please, Mother, though I am so weary and painfully slow right now, don't let indifference grip my heart. Let my Love grow more and more sensitive and quick to respond to Him Who has first loved me.

Wednesday, October 21

How inclined am I to "help" Our Father relocate me. How hastily I mumbled today at the thought of being placed with a bunch of physically handicapped. It would be crushing, like returning to St. John's without legs that can take little ones where they wish, and hands that can feed and dress [*others*], and without a back that can lift even those [*lighter*] than I. [*Virginia was recalling her two years at St. John's Hospital for Handicapped Children in Springfield, Illinois. While there she was still strong enough to be of assistance to other children, which she loved to do. The thought of being in that type of environment, without strength enough to be physically useful, was obviously very distressing to her.*]

Mother, I try hard to forget those former luxuries and press on to know only Jesus Christ and Him crucified. To have a living reminder of the past surrounding me every day would be crushing; but then do I not beg for this daily martyrdom? Yes, Mother, please take my confusion and mete from it only what is deserving of Our Father. And if, as I fear, you find nothing there for Him, please, I beg you, put it there yourself.

Thank you, Mother, for permitting these love notes from your little one. Somehow everything falls into its beautiful place when I bring it to your feet, and so happily I abandon everything here and rest in the security that your love wraps about me. Blessed be night that lies in expectation. Welcome to confusion's darkness, which prepares my poor soul for the dawn!

Thursday, October 22

I just returned from the Dairy Queen, where I ordered its largest Coke. Look, Mother, here's the cup of the gigantic "fifty-five cent-er." It's such fun to be a little one constantly bug-eyed among all the wonders Our Father sends, even mammoth Cokes. What little ones can make distinctions in regards to values? How foolish to try. I long to embrace each moment in such eagerness that I may squeeze from it all the tears and laughter hidden there to shape our Eternity.

Friday, October 23

Your little hobo is so tired tonight. Her path has been an exacting one today. Please don't find a note of complaint here, and if you do, sing but louder with me a joyous song of praise. My stomach is still grumbling, and the pain that I am feeling tonight is dull and constant. I'm weary, Mother, but I remember that through your loving kindness I live and die for another. With your embrace I whisper, "Where is the sting?" and slip into sleep's oblivion, knowing you won't leave me alone.

Saturday, October 24 (Feast of the Archangel Raphael)

Please send Raphael to assist a very weary hobo, to make her Love strong. All other weakness . . . I welcome.

Tuesday, October 27

Mother, I see today how you are helping me to stand with you beneath the Cross. You cannot remove the pain of it. That would be to remove the Cross, and never could I be a Little Sister without it. The pain is that one immortal *fiat*; the *fiat* is the pain. But somewhere in a region where not even joy nor anguish enter is the constant Presence of Christ, my Peace. I believe this with all my heart; please help my love to grow that my faith may increase and bound with joy till it is annihilated in Vision.

Friday, October 30

"What if this present were the world's last night?" I'd peck a note to you and die peacefully in your arms.

Sunday, November 1 (All Saints' Day)

With all those marked by the precious seal of the Cross, I unite myself in an oblation through Jesus to the glory of the

Father. It seems on this beautiful feast of Jesus Christ triumphant I could go on and on in this note to you, but exile keeps interrupting with weariness and pain, and a heart devoid of all but desire. Please transform my all into a hymn of glory for Divine Love. I ask much; teach me to ask for All. Mother of saints, please don't forget a sinner who loves you.

Wednesday, November 4

Only this morning I wrote to Ruth Arreche, telling her of a growing conviction that Jesus just isn't ready to move his little hobo now. Somehow I was happy just to tell her, happy in a true *fiat*, in the thought that I may stay a little longer with Sam to gather all his precious sufferings and with you and Jesus continue saving the world. NOTHING MUST BE WASTED. Every heartbeat seems to tell me so.

Mother, it's so wonderful to have this conviction I have tonight. Perhaps soon more precious little crosses of confusion will appear, familiar, nearly friendly, on this hobo's path to tell her it is Jesus' way. But for this sweet moment I rest a little in the sunset and dream of a Dawn.

Tuesday, November 10

Mother dear, Jesus wants me to learn of the desert. All day He's tried to tell me of it, of "Charlie," of mortification, of our blessed nakedness before our Creator. My heart is so slow to understand, but it is waiting for these lessons as the sands await water's refreshment, or blood's crimson robe.

Monday, November 16

I've been searching for a spot in which to spend a day in the desert, fool that I am. I live daily in the desert. Alone with God? Yes, so very alone, tossed into a sea of suffering and unhappiness and loneliness and cruelty and nagging persecution, just less than enough to make me feel a pride in this hourly martyrdom. It's good to be at Sam, in this little corner with Jesus, pecking a loving goodnight to Our Mother. This is Happiness. O to take every precious second and give it to Him! And now and then when the multitudes are a little quieter, to go aside and rest a while with Him.

Thursday, November 19

In watching "Dr. Kildare" on TV tonight, I heard Dr. Gillespie speaking of love. He mentioned what it meant to many, but to him it was simply *contentment*. It's time for rest now, for content. And it's Thursday night. "Can you not watch one hour with me?" my beloved Lord and Brother Jesus Christ asks. Can I not be content to sit at His feet, to gaze upon Him Crucified, Him Majestic, and be satisfied in the possession of Him and in being possessed by Him? Who could teach me better than a Mother to watch with her Son?

Saturday, November 21

Please thank Our Father for warmth this evening. At last my feet have circulation and my fingers are not blue. Please don't let us go through again the agonies we've endured the past two days. My jaws nearly locked shut this morning, something in my throat that made swallowing difficult, muscle spasms everywhere in my body, and another of those headaches I thought were gone. If I suffer so, what of these dear old folks? If my body was covered with "goose bumps," what of these with hardened arteries? Here is all the suffering the cold has caused my dear old folks, their comfort tonight and a plea that it may last to ease the fall of twilight's curtain.

Sunday, November 22

"Behold, I make all things new!" Yes, what was magnificent is no more, and what was little and vile He has assimilated in

Himself. O God, who is like You; please come in Your terrible majesty and let me not be one to tremble at Your approach. The Church's holy cycle draws to a close, and here we stand awaiting our Judge and our reward. "If You should keep a record of our transgressions, Lord, who could stand it?" Here is my poor heart. There is nothing there to please You but the Cross that has been eternally rooted therein. I know You look for nothing more than this, the sacred sign of our salvation. My Mother, please tend to it, and as you behold the poverty of the soil in which it is planted, water it with your precious tears that it grow tall enough to hold Jesus Christ and Him Crucified in the only Triumph.

Friday, November 27

Late last night I read a few words from "Charlie's" pen on the mercy of God, then tried the hitherto unsuccessful practice of keeping watch with Jesus Thursday night, the night of His anguish and loneliness. It seemed I could have stayed with Him all night. Was it gratitude or anguish or love or wonder that kept me there? Where will this broadening desire to imitate my little brother of the desert lead me? It isn't for me to ask, I know; please help me to follow faithfully this chosen path to Calvary, my only triumph. I am an infant who wouldn't comprehend the answers to the questions of my heart even if you gave them to me. Mother, I need you so; please show me Jesus. Though I must sleep now, please see that His Presence in the tabernacle of my very body is never lacking adoration.

Saturday, November 28

It's a few minutes after midnight, and Holy Mother Church has launched us into a new year of grace. O that the life of Christ in its entirety be lived in our hearts. During this holy season you'll be so dear to us as with you we wait in longing for, and joyous anticipation of, Christ. We are Christians-in-waiting; when will we be worthy to look upon God's Face? You alone can teach us this readiness. Please do, Mother.

Sunday, November 29

The bookcase where your beautiful image, The Rocking-chair Madonna, is usually enshrined, seems bare tonight. I've put that carving away till Christmas, and already I miss it. It's such an insignificant way of perceiving what so many feel as they await Christ, and how can I guess what their anguish is if they know not Him for Whom their heart cries? Still, I gather the cry of a world and bring it here to you tonight. In my heart is the tiny prayer that greeted me this morning as I leafed to the First Sunday of Advent in my missal. It's on a holy card I got at the Cape, beneath a picture of you holding Jesus, little ones playing at your feet. "Give us Jesus. *Donnez-nous Jesus!*" Amen.

Tuesday, December 1

As of seven o'clock this evening, my little brother "Charlie" has been dead forty-eight years. But how can I speak of death as I happily think of him who is so vibrantly alive to me today? This evening, after I'd finished Holy Mother Church's night prayers in my short Breviary, I stayed there at the feet of our Eucharistic King to await the hour of "Charlie's" defeat, identical with his triumph. It seemed he was with me there, again, kneeling before Christ, his hands tied, a gun at his head, waiting for death and reviewing his life. How forcefully the words he once wrote returned, "All my plans turn out to be mere bits of paper." Yes, my heart whispered, I understand, "Charlie." I weigh my deeds with my intentions and cringe at the imbalance; I weep, I resolve, and I fall. This is my life. One seed has fallen and blossomed in the desert; another throws herself to the sand and begs them to cover her that she keep him company there and in Eternity. Little Sister Death, bring night upon us, and Christ's Resurrection.

Tuesday, December 15

It's so small, this sleepy little love ya, but it's my all that I bring to you, Mother. Now that I've placed it in your tender care, I abandon my weary self to slumber and dreams of dawn and newness and strength in Him Who has called Himself our Light.

Sunday, December 20

My beautiful Jean was here this evening. The comfort of her presence was so soothing that I fell asleep. It was a wonderful visit, for there we were together, pretending nothing more than what we were, wanting nothing more, content. And if this gave way to the weariness that nags me these days, I knew I needn't apologize. We are waiting for Christ, and if we slumber, the tiny Mighty One can send a choir of angels to waken us, and in glad confidence I know He will.

Tuesday, December 22

Only this afternoon did I get my Christmas greetings in the mail, all 225 of them. So many words, yet please guide my loved ones to read therein but one tiny Word which you hold. Mother, it's terribly late, and I truly must be scooting. Just had to peck a few words and love ya's to you, and tell you how anxious I am to see your Baby's Face. Please prepare me for it.

Sunday, January 3, 1965
[After Christmas at St. Meinrad's]

Here's your little hobo, Mother dear, consoled and happy that you are here to receive all that I am and LOVE IT. Yes, that is the mystery I'd be a fool to try to comprehend; I believe.

Where can I begin my account of the blessings with which my poverty has been adorned these past days? And how am I to know even if they are lovelier than those subtle blessings that weigh upon my heart here at Sam? It's not for me to be concerned. I simply bring all to you that you may make it somewhat presentable to Jesus. Surely after all is in your hands I'd be a fool to have any further concern for it. Yes, I AM so often a fool. But YOU LOVE ME. O for the littleness to let myself be loved!

My beautiful Hobo Haven, it was so warm this visit; the promise of spring seemed in the air and the rain and the anticipation. Never has His Majesty come so jubilantly. He Who came last year to show me His weakness invited me this time to fling myself upon the consolation of His strength. His image in the Abbey Church kept inviting my gaze. It seemed He wanted to stoop and with one hand scoop me up to hear forever the beating of His Heart. Please direct my anguished joy to Him that at the end of exile I may come upon His Majesty and find the sweetness of Home.

Wednesday, January 6

My beautiful Mother wrapped in silence, please let every person be a living Epiphany to me, and by some inscrutable design of our Father, me to them.

Saturday, January 9

"Craving for a deeper knowledge of existentialism and phenomenology?" In reading these words today's mail brought, I smiled with relief at my sufficient, if meager, education. Why must all these things concern us, since John has told us in all simplicity that God is LOVE?

Sunday, January 17

Please accept the peck of a hobo whose heart you've taught to beat for only Jesus.

O Mother, after not having written for a week, my prayer is a maze of disconnected joys and heartaches so inseparable the mere thought of trying to put a semblance of them on paper is humorous. And I love your smile.

Wednesday afternoon Velma and I rode to Indianapolis to enjoy the movie "My Fair Lady" with Father Keith. It was so uplifting, and even if I'd not found it so, Father's delighted giggle would have made it so for me. Poor Eliza, how I can sympathize with her, I who am anything but a fair lady, with a foot hanging out one side of the wheelchair, my head at the other, arms waving, giggles or tears, shoes flying through the air. O but the grace of seeing oneself thus and finding Our Father's sense of humor, please thank Him for this.

Such a blessedly high pile of letters awaited my return, and with Jesus' strength I know I shall be able to continue giving His Love to my growing list of correspondents. It seems your little hobo will truly earn her name these coming weeks and months. Never have invitations poured in like this. They are all longing for Jesus; please don't let me disappoint them.

Thursday, January 21

Mother dear, please put in the poverty called my heart the same desires as those which fill your own. But I know it's too small for that. Rather take my heart, my all, remembering how thoroughly I belong to you, and let my love and my life be your own.

Wednesday, January 27

Mother, I beg not to disappoint your Son. O to love as Jesus loves, as much as Jesus loves, with His very Love! To love to the point of placing infinite trust in everyone, to give them something to which their goodness will respond. They've been waiting so long for someone to expect big things of them. Don't let me stunt their growth by my limited expectations, but let my demands on them be just as fantastic as Jesus'.

All is quiet now; it is precious Night. Please let me hear you speak again His Name.

Friday, January 29

There is but one phrase my heart keeps shouting as I come to these precious moments of giving my day to you, Mother: "Live, Jesus!" Please accomplish this miracle in the poor heart that finds its consolation in your tender care. How truly you are my hope.

Monday, February 1

Here is my day, Mother, in it nothing of which I can be proud, thank God. Success is so subtle, failure sometimes so prominent. And who am I to presume to judge either? I just hope against all that is in me that somehow in my life mysterious victories glorify Our Father. In simplicity, I bring you today.

Tuesday, February 2 (Feast of the Presentation)

Another feast, and because I love you so, Mother, it's been a glorious day. How often have I paused to thank God for this love of you that rejoices my heart? It, too, is a grace, a tremendous gift I treasure. And the more precious it becomes to me, the greater the love that floods the poverty known as my heart. There is so much good in my life I must fail to recognize, great graces such as this one. What I am yet ignorant of please include in that perpetual *Magnificat* your soul sings for your graces and all of ours.

How many have ever recognized the Light of the world in my eyes? I'm glad this is hidden from me, that I be not tempted to despair. I do know that MY eyes have seen Him. I hold those precious images in my heart. Please let me never let them go till together we are plunged into the Beatific Vision.

Thursday, February 4

More and more must I surrender human consolations to kneel at the feet of Jesus Crucified. He is so silent. I ramble on and on of suffering as I sit so cozily at His feet. Make me be quiet that I may better realize HIS pain and that my only suffering be that He must suffer so. He is so terribly silent, yet doesn't His form stretched out there scream all I need to hear and yet more my heart hasn't yet opened to?

Wednesday, February 17

The stars are out again, always, though daylight still fills the sky. And when the stars appear soon I shall laugh at them, as I do so often. For there they sparkle and thousands of little souls look upon them. Yet, as Father Lucien once reminded me, "Not a star that floats through space will ever see God face-to-face." And so I love the stars, and mostly how I love to laugh with them at their brilliance and my own humble dignity.

I've missed these notes to you each night, Mother, though we've surely shared all things in our Beloved Jesus. There are no joys without Him, and my precious joys in Him are mine only because *you* show me where His Love is hiding in all life's riddles. Please go always with your little one become hobo for Love's sake, and make Jesus always at least a loved and frequent distraction in the multitudes, and when daylight is gone and the pressure of the multitude is eased, though never forgotten, let blessed night wrap me in Him and Him in me.

Thursday, February 18

Just as it would be most unhealthy to rest always or to be in constant motion, please, beautiful Woman, assure us that you are directing your little ones' growth that we continue on our way to God without hesitating to determine if our stride be too fast or too slow.

Saturday, February 20

Please fill me so with the Word of God that, whenever I speak, others may somehow hear Jesus' Name, and, when I am silent, the light that is He shine from me, though I'll be aware of neither in myself.

Tuesday, February 23

Please, Mother, help me to open my heart to everyone that Jesus, too, may slip in, almost unnoticed, and stay because He finds traces of you there inviting.

Friday, February 26

Did I ever tell you I love you? I must tell you again, because each time it's from a new depth.

Saturday, February 27

Tonight I see but the picture of Jesus I just put on our bulletin board. My King in bitter anguish and intense pain. His body is but one royal red wound as He says at one and the same time, "I'm thirsty," and, "Take and eat." He is drained that we be filled. How can I go on bringing Him but emptiness? Yes, in childlike stupidity and presumption I beg to be crucified with Jesus. The only semblance I see is that darkness surrounds the two of Us. Blessed be my darkest hour in which, with Jesus, I shall somehow save the world. Crucify me!!!

Sunday, February 28

"Let's go to Jerusalem. . . ." Jesus' invitation leaves no doubt that He makes His Hour, His bitterest defeat and His eternal victory, ours. Though my heart already weeps at all He must endure, my soul sings joyous pilgrim songs. Through Him, with Him and in Him please show me how to truly say, "OUR FATHER."

Monday, March 1

Now is the month during which we remember especially your dear spouse, Joseph. Please help me to know better this month him who is so dear to you. Whisper Nazareth's secrets to me, and place in my poor heart, where I wish to make a Nazareth for Jesus today especially, that holy silence of listening love that enveloped your Holy Family.

Tuesday, March 2

This morning I typed a few liturgical improvements for Father ____. I'm so weary of hearing every change ridiculed, of having the "mistakes" of the [*Second Vatican*] Council thrown at me each time Father enters, which is several times a day. I want to run from it; please teach me instead to make this, too, a means of sanctification, for if these uncharitable thoughts persist I shall surely be the least Christian among those whose unchristian actions revolt me.

Wednesday, March 3

Today begins the sacred season of Lent. Mother, please be incessant with your little ones these days that they learn nothing but Jesus Christ and Him crucified, and triumphant. Lead us in the Way of the Cross and whisper to us of Him Who is Himself the Way and the Truth and the Light, and your Son and our very Brother.

My heart will rest only in the truth that is Jesus. Let me care enough that beads of blood burst from my forehead, yet in the same instant let my soul thunder its loyalty to the Father's Will. For even in this desolation peace lies there, in His Holy will. Though my desires and my needs are so vastly different, let the heat of Jesus' Love melt them to one longing for Him. Let only Jesus be my treasure, that my heart cease breaking at being torn in so many directions. Only Jesus!

Friday, March 5

A little seed of the desert begs you to water her and prays that she become strong. The Word of God, beaten, dying, says,

"I speak with her face-to-face, and when she has sight of the Lord, it is not by means of parable and image." But this vision shakes the very foundations of my soul. My Love is Crucified. When O when will my strength be such that I can stand beneath the Cross with you, unwavering, and with Him will His Death and the most perfect glorification of Our Father?

Sunday, March 7

Our Jesus had endured temptation in His tremendous love, desiring to be like us in all things, in the end even heaping upon Himself all guilt. By His bruises we are healed; by His temptation we have the tremendous strength to withstand all satanic power. Mortification is but the natural course of one who has placed his treasure in heaven. Please obtain this grace for me, Mother, during this sacred season.

Tuesday, March 9

Mother, I am lonely. Please hear no note of complaint in my confession, for I understand more and more that when the infinity of God bends to draw one closer to Love all other light is obscured. Only in His Light do we see light, yet my eyes are not yet attuned to the celestial. I'm just waiting. During these sacred days of Lent, Holy Mother Church keeps praying that we learn to look to heaven to find our true treasure and happiness. I need this lesson; Mother, your little one comes to you to learn Jesus, only Jesus.

Wednesday, March 10

"I did not understand until His words took living forms before my eyes." Gibran [*Kahlil Gibran, poet, artist*]. These living forms are everywhere. O that I might see. His words lie forgotten in a hospital bed, misunderstood beneath the worn trappings of a religious habit, or perhaps thoroughly unheard by ears tuned to so much less than Jesus. Since the Word became flesh, I have no excuse not to hear. His own know His voice; please make me at last His own.

Saturday, March 13

What tremendous things are expected from one to whom ALL has been given? Please beg for me the inexhaustible mercy of Our Father, and through some miracle of divine grace let Him be pleased with me. My back, arms, legs, neck are a precious ache; let them but be the cry of my heart for Jesus.

Tuesday, March 16

A postcard from Father Eugene! It's been so long. I do believe the little phrase about no news being good news, but a little word, knowledge that he is well, that's good, too. All that comes from our Father is good; please teach me to recognize His kindness in everything.

This afternoon, Daddy and I discussed our approaching trip to my lovely Hobo Haven. The mere anticipation is thrilling, just as all life is thrilling in the dawn of Eternity. Please let these days of rest at this spot, where Love invites us to come aside a little while in Its warmth, but drive me on to yet greater darkness and weariness and pain that I may at last come Home to you.

Wednesday, March 17

Jesus dies, darkness enfolds us, and, miracle of prodigality, we are saved. O my soul, love this night because you know there will be day.

Thursday, March 18

With what abundance my poor little cup overflowed this afternoon in spending with Father Sal precious moments that ran into hours, and into eternity. Father asked me to fill a tape for him with some of these notes to you, poetry and other writings. You know how I want to run from all recorders. But there was the request of someone I love, the opportunity of pleasing him through an activity so distasteful. And then there was nothing I wanted more than to put the message of a fool on tape that it be ridiculed and perhaps sometimes become itself an instrument of divine grace. Our own pleasure is forgotten when Divine Providence indicates to us the way to Our Father's glory.

Friday, March 19

Please, sweetheart of Joseph, greet him today in the name of all God's People. His name has become nearly synonymous with Nazareth. Dare I beg to enter into these hidden mysteries? Yes, a child does not calculate what she deserves but runs in total confidence to express every desire, trusting in her mother's love to determine and fulfill her needs.

Again and again I beg you to teach me to pray, to love. And what there is lacking in my heart — everything Jesus wishes to find there — please pour into it from your infinite treasury, "that Christ may look into my heart and see your soul reflecting there and I may hear His voice call, 'Mary!' as He looks at me and finds He is at home."

Saturday, March 20

Remembering, anticipating, how much of my life is wasted because I know not how to live in the eternal Present of God. There is so very much I need to learn. Please, Mother, help me.

Sunday, March 21

There is lodged within my throat an ache, and I can't determine whether it is grief or joy. It seems to be both. What song might I sing to set it free and let it wing its way to God? Please let me fling myself into His hands at last in the everlasting tremendous echo of your *Magnificat*.

Thursday, March 25 (Feast of the Annunciation)

Hail Mary, full of grace, the Lord is with you! Mother, what must it be like to be FULL of grace, to have the Life of God coursing through every fiber of your body and your soul? To be so clothed in simplicity's beauty that God Himself should come to you, a Beggar asking that He come in and don your flesh and be refreshed with your blood. With the highest angels I salute you, not shy that my voice mar their heavenly hymn, for you are MY Mother. Not even they can make such a boast. Please distract attention to my unworthiness by permitting an echo of your *fiat's* eternal roar in my heart.

This was my very first "day in the desert" as recommended in the Jesus-Caritas Fraternity. I was rather anxious, for I've never been alone in God. Somehow I'd anticipated an aridity for lack of friends or books, etc. But instead, a cloud of peace descended and I was in God and He in me. That was sufficient. Not a sound did I hear but two cars that passed and Jesus' whisper, wherein I pulled from the inaudible message the word "Peace" and a kiss that thrilled my weary heart. Fear that I might sleep with such inactivity vanished quickly in the thrilling activity of Love. And now I know that a little sister goes not to a desert but, in contrast to her usual environment, an OASIS. Please thank Our Father for today, and for all days of desert in which to remember His refreshment and anticipate the stream of living water that awaits us in the Promised Land. I was made aware of how truly my little sisters here in Kokomo have helped me enter into the spirit of Jesus-Caritas. Now I return to Sam begging NOT that I be taken from the world, but that I take the world with me always to Jesus.

Friday, March 26

Your very weary little one begs to be refreshed in blessed night that nothing hinder her from rushing into tomorrow morning's dawn.

Sunday, April 4

Good evening, Mother dear, and the most tremendous "love ya" my poverty can fling.

Last night, Father Keith paid us a visit at suppertime. After our meal was finished, my poor heart was invited to go aside a few minutes to converse with Jesus. O blessed opportunity, I don't wish to forget a word. I consulted Father concerning my Easter promises, and he told me to do as Jesus wishes. Mother, in the confusion that envelops my life these days, I long to know Jesus' wishes. This knowledge alone will break the chains of darkness that bind me. Am I spiritually immobile? I don't know. Jesus leads me; only in this remembrance can I get even a fitful rest.

With what wisdom spoke my little brother last night. Never have I suspected that I am plagued with "guilt," yet I see now that he is right. This has been and will be the burden of my life. And here, where I see cruelty day after day, and live again and again all the terrifying pains of my childhood, it is fostered. I hate it here; I can hardly stand the abuses inflicted on those around me. They peel off again the scab that hides the deep wound in my heart, and it can never heal. And I hate my own intolerance of these circumstances. Never can I escape this agony. Please halt my running. Let me reach Gethsemane and see there my Little Brother sprawled upon a rock, unable for a moment to rise because He is crushed by the guilt of all evil. Yes, how I pray that this cup pass from me, but in the same moment it is raised to my lips because it is the Father's Will. O to drink it to the dregs! Father asks me to be truthful. With poor, cowardly Pilate I ask, "What is truth?" and you show me again, only Jesus. These indignations, these anguished cries that I muffle day after day, yes to divulge them is to reveal my weakness, to lower others' opinions of me. Yet these are me; what right have I to hide them? Mother, you see how much confidence Father Keith has placed in me in revealing to me this precious knowledge. Let me not betray his trust, Jesus', please.

Tuesday, April 6

O to draw all my brothers and sisters closer, to hide among them and to know that they "fill up what is lacking" in my sacrifice, that I may prepare myself worthily for my coming promises to Jesus! Please, full of grace, fill me.

Heard word from Father Lucien today concerning my books of letters to you. Please let me know just what you wish done with them, so that when we "talk this over over an Easter egg," we'll please you and Jesus with our decision.

Today books speak to me. It is good to hear them again. Please help me to be patient in God's silence. St. John of the Cross says, "The healing of love is to hurt and wound once more that which has been hurt and wounded already, until the soul comes to be wholly dissolved in the wound of love." Please pray that I be wounded, that my Hour come at last. And beg my God, the Eternal, risen from the dead, to come to bring back to life the child in me.

Monday, April 12

My precious little sisters Jean, Lulu, and Ruth have just left this corner. We've shared matzo, a cup of wine, St. John's poignant account of the Last Supper, and finally an hour's watch with Jesus in His lonely anguish. When I see my family gather thus, I know more and more clearly what Jesus spoke of when He told us to live in His Love. Please, Mother, make your children vibrantly alive.

Tuesday, April 13

Please, Mother, plunge your little one into all Holy Week's agony and glory her poverty can withstand.

CONSECRATION

Our beloved Lord and Brother Jesus Christ, you have rolled away the stone and overcome my heart. Today I consecrate anew, through our Mother, my poor littleness, singing with the joyous hope that You will fill up what is lacking in my holocaust and remove from me all that is not You, that Our Father be well pleased.

I am not a lovely "sermon" on the Holy Gospel, but please let my folly be Your glorification. Make me content even with being discontented, my joy the remembrance that my Beloved is eternally happy in the bosom of Our Father.

It is Your little hobo who comes to You with such boundless confidence. Please keep me. Amen.

Little Virginia of Jesus, 4-18-65.

In foreground, left to right: brother Jimmy and Virginia; behind Virginia: their father, Oliver

eight

APRIL 25, 1965, TO SEPTEMBER 8, 1966

*V*irginia and Quentin Colgan meet for the first time on Wednesday of Holy Week, 1965. During that stay at St. Meinrad's, Virginia entrusts her "Letters" to Quentin. Her weakening condition results in the loss of her voice, and she experiences several lengthy hospital stays. Tragically, Virginia is molested by a priest who served as an occasional chaplain at "Good Sam." As her physical condition deteriorates, her desire for "Home" increases. She makes several more trips to St. Meinrad's during this time. She writes: "I am filled by many and drained by many, but if I am Jesus', how silly to try to determine just what He's doing with me at present. I do know that when I seek to enjoy my fullness, I am parched; when my brothers and sisters come thirsting, I am a fountain that will not be exhausted. O thank God! Sometimes I want to cry out in anguish. Cry what? I don't know, for I can NEVER ask to be returned to my former selfishness. Please lead me on, and if my foolishness cries in anguish, then still lead me on till there is nothing of mine to cry but only Jesus."

+
LOVE

Sunday, April 25, 1965

Mother dear, never has there seemed so much to tell you, and never has the humiliation of wrenching words from inexpressible mysteries been so poignant. All the way to the monastery I shared the parched lips and Heart of Jesus. Even my tongue was hardened and dressed in a thirsty color. And though I've built up my bodily moisture somewhat, still I thirst. When will it be finished? Because it is Jesus' I beg for added moments or days or years to call it mine and please Our Father and save souls. O but Mother, I thirst.

One there was who raised a saturated sponge to my lips. Strange it was, and wonderful. We'd never met before. At first I was to him just another stranger, condemned to hang as so many others. Almost before he knew what he was doing he offered me a drink, and through some miracle I felt his sponge soak from me any last drops of moisture that might have been found there, and in the saturation of his heart I am satisfied. It was finished. I went that he might have Life and have it more abundantly; and only death can grant this. I went to the monastery to die for him, though I had never known him before. And now he lives a part of me forever. Frater Quentin, do you know how I love you? Is this not the majestic joy of motherhood during the anguish of childbirth? I am not concerned with just what I am experiencing. God is and I am, and darkness is sweet.

Why is it that I feel so stripped? Why am I screaming for the God Who has abandoned me and in the same breath abandoning myself into His hands? I am such a paradox I can no longer endure myself. Help me to fix my heart on only Jesus. Long before I'd gone to St. Meinrad's this time, Jesus kept telling me I was to forget the consolation that usually awaits me there. But never did I suspect that even the presence of those so precious to me would become as nothing. Mother, please see that my brother Quentin is filled; I am so emptied.

This morning I left without goodbyes. Faith tells me this was the most precious of all visits there. Please let my heart answer, "Yes, I know."

Saturday, May 1

Saturday mornings I dust furniture and pictures and crawl on my hands and knees to dust-mop the floor of my pretty little corner. It's so little, yet probably the most taxing manual labor I perform all week. And if I am tired when I am through, it is a participation in Our Father's act when He looks upon the world He has made and sees that it is good and rests. Everything in this exile is a shadowed participation in His glory. If I should forget just how intimate is His Love, please remember to place me irrevocably in His hands. He will draw me so close till the beating of His Sacred Heart and mine are beyond distinction and He is my Life.

Sunday, May 2

"Do you love Me? Feed My sheep," Jesus says. I do have a little, but what is such poverty to do for so many? If I keep it for myself I shall go hungry. But if I run to give it to Him for the multitude they will be filled and I, too, as I banquet in the midst of the least of them and find Jesus looking their way as He speaks of the greatest in His Kingdom. Here I am among the least of His little ones, the useless and abandoned ones. I love Jesus; please help me to fulfill the one proof He demands of my love.

Tuesday, May 4

I must be on my way, must be willing, for the sake of the Gospel, to go to the ends of the earth and to live till time is no more if Jesus should ask this of me. I am not worthy of His asking anything of me. Yet in His tremendous Love He lets His Sacred Humanity repose in His Father's glory, and chooses instead the weakness that I am to accomplish His mission. If I live in His Love, even my tears are precious, and in complete humility I can become an Alleluia from head to toe. My brothers and sisters are safe because I ask that they be so. And a God Who is Love cannot ignore my request for them. I go my way, to Calvary, that they may have Life, abundantly.

Wednesday, May 5

It was such a burst of sunshine to pick up the phone this morning and hear Father Keith's voice. If I sport independence and brag to myself of detachment, one moment like that this morning proves me such a phony. O the happiness of talking to him, the lovableness of his wit, his precious way of scolding and encouraging. Thank you for such a precious little brother.

Monday, May 10

On this the 23rd anniversary of my birth into this good earth, and also of the day on which the waters of Baptism let Our Father smile because He saw that this bit of creation was good (reminded Him of His Son), I come to thank you, Mother, so insufficiently yet sincerely, for the gift of Life and the Way and the Truth. Mother, I'm sorry I cannot write a lovely letter tonight. I long to bring you SOMETHING of loveliness, but right now there is none in me. It is painful to give the likes of me to you. Yet Jesus has loved me and what is there to respond but, "Lord, I give. . ."?

Friday, May 14

All is still; it is wondrous night. A pleasant breeze flutters my curtains and the curtain, in turn, rubs gently against my precious Rocking-chair Madonna, causing the lovely carving to become alive to me in the soothing motions of Motherhood. I find myself in your arms, rocking, abandoned, content, yours.

Sunday, May 23

Wearily yet zealously I greet you this evening, my precious Mother. I've just returned from a week with the Sisters at Maria Stein, Ohio. It has been a stained-glass experience, but then so is life in general. And though my childishness can glimpse a little of its beauty already, there is still so much I fail to comprehend because I've not let Jesus take such possession of me that I may see with the eyes of Wisdom the hundred million miracles that are lovingly performed within and around me each day. For those that I see, and especially for those I do not recognize, please hide this *Magnificat* in your own eternally exultant echo.

Wednesday morning I was speaking to one angelic sister when soon you, Mother, became the object of our wonderful little exchange. It seemed the more I spoke of you the greater this already great love of you became until my heart could hardly withstand further increase. There grew an intense physical pain in my right chest so great that at last I had to cease speaking, and with some flimsy excuse rush to my room and rest a little. O Love too immense for my mortal frame, please consume me. But I am not worthy; please burn all self, all waste material, from me, and be the Life and death of me.

Wednesday, May 26

A loving little hello, Mother, after a precious day of love. How can I express my joyous gratitude at being with Father Keith today? A trip to the clinic necessary? I didn't think so. But my heart needed the time with him, the shared experiences and simply the joyous pleasure mere being together gives.

Doc was pretty special; please tell him I think so. We had such a nice chat. Strange that he was so sincerely interested in "my work." I answered his incessant questions almost boldly. And once again I was standing aside, amusedly listening to myself. I was telling Doc the simple, beautiful truth, of hoboing and correspondence and the appropriateness of living in an old people's home, and praying. And perhaps for the first time I wasn't simultaneously making excuses for my vocation. So convinced was I of my vocation that if he should have branded me lazy and tried to convince me of some other responsibilities, I would have been undisturbed. But this was not his attitude; it was respect and a request to be remembered in my prayers. Tonight I offer his loving kindness, his curiosity, his respect, the collar repair he took care of from his own pocket, that he continue to grow in his love for us little guys, for Jesus.

Father Keith and I have just returned to Kokomo, and though he's gone, how truly he remains, a part of me forever, and I his, the least of his flock, the one I hope he will choose first to lay upon the Altar in sacrifice for the others. Will you tell him of something he must have noticed incessantly today, my poor but undying love?

Thursday, May 27

Yes, once there were green fields kissed by the sun whose warmth permeated me. Once. Green fields to remind me of harvest and make me smile. Now this little hobo's duty is but to plant seeds, to dig beneath what seems barren and put there a spark of Eternal Life. Then I must be on my way, leaving all fruit behind for the Conqueror to whom I send but one request, "Thy Kingdom come."

Sunday, May 30

"And when the blessings are all used up, then simply say: AMEN." [*Kahlil*] Gibran. To all that has happened, to all that is, to all that will be: Amen!

Monday, May 31

To what other "Queen" might I run so happily and find always an affectionate embrace? With little Thérèse I'm ALMOST inclined to think, "We are more fortunate than she, because . . . she had no Blessed Virgin to love."

Wednesday, June 2

How inclined we mortals are to give our God the last fruits, the leftovers. This morning I had a quite convenient schedule worked out: The Eucharist, coffee, three quick letters, and in what time was left, moments with Jesus before the day's hoboing began. But Divine Kindness brought me to our little chapel, then put our elevator out of order till 9:30. All that time to be in the precious company of my Beloved. Please thank Him for always frustrating my insufficient plans.

Thursday, June 10 (Ascension Thursday)

This afternoon we were gathered together in one place (Jean, Lulu, Mary, Jane, Peg and Ruby with their little sister) to receive the Holy Spirit and all His gifts. How else can we express our gratitude for these unless we employ them, abandon ourselves to His direction, be filled to overflowing so that others may drink from our cup, and with our happiness in Jesus renew the face of the earth? Please make us gracious receivers, little servant girls of God.

Friday, June 25

O precious one in whom the Sacred Heart of Jesus was formed and took its first omnipotent beat, and whose blood poured itself into that Heart that it in turn pour it upon us and we be truly called your children: we love you. Jesus exchanged His Heart with St. Margaret Mary, and thereafter she was never relieved of the precious pain in her side. Please let the incessant heartache I bear be this, that Jesus has given me His Heart and my littleness cannot contain its immensity, and in its lack of universality reels but, O please, does not skip a beat.

It's been two weeks since I last had the happy opportunity to peck a "love ya" to you, Mother. There is lots to tell you, yet words seem to flee. Let only that Word God spoke through you to me remain.

The retreat? Yes, it was the best ever. I don't know just what Jesus is accomplishing in me these days. It's not for a little one to ask. O the tremendous peace of knowing that I am only because through me Jesus wishes to manifest His Love to my brothers and sisters. No conference in my memory, only moments of weariness somehow overcome and others not overcome, this was my retreat. I AM that others might have life, abundantly. How or when is not for me to ask.

This ring, which even now I am fingering, who can know the totality of its significance? Least of all did I comprehend that as I ran to my Spouse, Jesus Christ, last Easter. Never did I run to Him with such abandon, and never could He have taken me before in such entirety. Now I have nothing, till one of my brothers or sisters stretches a hand to me. I stand there speechless; how can I tell them what utter poverty I am? I needn't tell them, for somehow there is enough to fill their cup. There's always enough for them. To this hope I cling. "God alone is sufficient." Then my heart wants to cry to them for help. It wants to tell them of poverty they'll never expect here. But why? Out of these depths I cry to God. Only He would endure my voice. But "before ever a word is on my lips, He knows the whole of it." Please hush me.

Saturday, June 26

How sweet to return to the routine, the security, of Nazareth. Rising while everything is still a-tingle with freshness, the simplicity of the Supreme Sacrifice, the pecking of my typewriter, the boost of an afternoon nap, even a bit of music on TV this evening, and finally this note to you and quiet with Jesus and abandon in Our Father's arms. What day would not thrill your little one? Only that on which she refuses to listen and open her eyes and live.

Tuesday, June 29

To love is to hope in another forever. That's a long time, Mother. It is impossible; but with Jesus' Love this and how much more am I capable of? Yes, charity begins at home, and because I am a little hobo, home is everywhere. Everywhere my love must BEGIN. Every minute is my failure and my beginning; this thought alone drives away discouragement. Please watch over a beginner.

Saturday, July 3

"He who plants kindness gathers love." Please, Mother, teach me to be kind and bury this little seed in the specific desert Jesus wishes for me, and let Him come soon to reap many and great lovers of Him.

Sunday, July 4

Please help me to shower upon others a bit of that exquisite kindness Our Father smiles upon me.

Tuesday, July 6

Twice today our elevator was out of order, and once yesterday and the day before. It's so often; please aid Sam. Our funds must be quite low. It is at times like these that the Old Boy keeps throwing suggestions at me like, "Perhaps they'll close the place. Besides, three years is much too long for you to be here. You're young and already throwing away precious years. Do something. Make it so that others NEED YOU. . . ." On and on he goes, and I with him till my foolish thoughts halt and I know that the labors of those who work under poverty of means are blessed also, a hundredfold. No one sees our harvest, for one cannot number souls. They're for Jesus alone.

Thursday, July 8

Just a few minutes ago, as I made the long trek from here to the John and back again, with tired arms that make it twice the journey, I found in my heart one incessant prayer. "Lord, he who sees me sees my brother also!" Tonight I AM this prayer, and I know that I cannot tumble into the strong arms of Our Father without taking with me each brother and sister He's given me. Please hasten me into my nightie; I'm impatient to abandon the world to God!

Friday, July 9

Among today's letters are three from disturbed friends. Their needs, their demands are so great it frightens. But I rest assured that for them I am strong and filled. Let them lean, for I am securely fastened to Jesus' Cross.

Tuesday, July 13

Agony, ecstasy, is there really any difference since Jesus is crucified? I do know that at Easter time I plunged myself into my Father's arms as never before, and nothing is or will be the same. God took me at my word. Such respect He has for His creatures. Now I implore the self-respect to know how irrevocable is the giving away of my heart and to kiss this ring that is the symbol of my servitude to total freedom.

Thursday July 15

After I've been disappointed, hurt and disappointed again, please let the flame of my hope in those I love but brighten.

That is the way Our Father seems to love me, and how fittingly Piety demands that I look upon my brothers and sisters and do likewise.

Monday, July 19

"They are your masters and you will find them terribly exacting masters. . . . It is only by feeling your love that the poor will forgive you for your gifts." Jerry, the poor unlovable one, I've just taken him a candy bar. He eats like one famished; he is hungry. Even decent meals are reserved here for the likable. Does he forgive me my gifts, the candy bars my friends bring and the roll I save from my own tray that he not lie awake hungry? Does he feel my love? Have I truly risen above being the self-congratulatory gift-giver to being the gift? Please ask my brothers to forgive my gift, to forgive me.

Tuesday, July 20

Who am I to presume to judge my friends' needs, I who know not my own? But please don't let my ignorance send them away hungry.

Thursday, July 22

Mother, teach me to exercise my womanliness. It is not for me to choose "the best part." Too many times each day you direct my prayer, "Father, I abandon myself into Your hands. Do with me what You will." I know that whatever part my Father chooses for me is the best part. And it will not be taken from me, please, even by my foolish self.

Friday, July 23

Heat, cold, fatigue, work, laughter, friendship, rest, all life is O so precious because God became man. He lived and made life worth living.

Saturday, July 24

Routine, the sweet little things of Nazareth I've loved each day. Thank you, Mother. In simplicity alone are discovered mysteries unsuspected by the wise. Now your little hobo must be on her way. Where? I know little about the paths from which Jesus calls, but they all lead to Calvary, to that throne which alone is worthy of homage, to torture, betrayal, poverty, death, to abundant Life for those for whom I've come. Please don't let my hesitance, my unworthiness, keep them waiting. My eyes are upon Jesus and I run!

Friday, July 30

A breathless Hi, Mother. I've just returned from Fort Wayne, where I spent a few days at the Villa [*orphanage*]. Yes, they were good, filled with memories of the only happy days I knew in childhood. Renewed acquaintances, new loves, souls,

Virginia out hoboing

souls, and souls. And Jesus' vocation is mine, that they may have life abundantly. Father, glorify Your Son!

My little retreat, and five days of thanksgiving. You see, we must even thank God for permitting us to say thank you. Now who would be so foolish as to try to get even with a Love such as that?! (Me.)

Saturday, July 31

Please Mother, in the grind of exhaustive hoboing or crushing routine, make me truly one with the Beloved Who calls Himself the Bread of Life.

Monday, August 9

Just now I've put in place the contents of my knapsack, and here I am for those precious moments with you my poor heart needs so. Mother, please assure me again that you can love such as me, that you, too, anticipate these precious chats. It's so hard to imagine your love of me, but you know I do believe in that love. It is the last spark in my life. Everything else seems so cold, but what matter? You are, Mother, and no minute of my life is devoid of beauty. Every fiber of my weakness calls you blessed, Mother.

Now I've deposited everything here, Mother, and am here limp, ready to be tossed forever into the strong hands of Our Father. That is the meaning of Good Night.

Wednesday, August 11

One precious goodie I must share with you, Mother dear. I share because I love you too much not to. The welfare lady was such an angel. After two hours of filling out her extremely detailed paperwork, she must still make another trip to finish. Yet how graciously she told me so; even her face said she'd be happy to give me yet more of her precious schedule. What was most delightful was that right in the midst of all the tiring data there was a space in which she was to list my *hobbies*. She smiled and without further consideration wrote, "PEOPLE."

Friday, August 13

I'm so tired, Mother, and so yours.

Sunday, August 15

Here I am at Sam beginning a third year as Father Keith's co-missionary. Something in me rebels at having been here so long, cries that I'm too young to consider an old people's home anything like permanent for me. And something in my more sensible self tells me I am just where I belong. Queen of peace, please remember that I'm yours. Lifetimes are very indefinite considerations. But today is to be accepted, every little particle of it, and lived to the fullest. Father Keith's red rose must some-day open wide, be utterly spent. And the proper time is now and the place here, anywhere I am put. What flower ever trans-planted herself? Please send me sunshine and rain, and most of all sing when I whimper so Jesus won't hear my complaint.

Monday, August 16

I had a request this evening, Mother. I wanted to make a worthy plea that you teach me that respect, that dauntless kind-ness each man has a right to. Instead my head is reeling from this increased medication. I'm so tired fighting it. Please take the rest of your little tippler, who has all day been leaning against the Son.

Wednesday, August 18

For the priest who graced my little corner this afternoon, for my precious missionary, for the newly ordained, for those whose burdens have dulled their zeal, for priests whose health prevents their offering the Holy Sacrifice, for those imprisoned, for those ignoring the sacred character their Ordination has placed indelibly upon them, for those called tonight to carry home a lost sheep, for priests whose burdens keep them awake, for those sleeping over the Breviary they well intended to finish, for all priests, your priests, I peck tonight's note, Mother dear.

Thursday, August 19

Precious night, Thursday night. May I not watch one hour with Jesus, or if not an hour at least a little while? My people here are resting; the night is comfortingly cool. I'll hop into my nightie now and kneel here for a while with Jesus, the burden of all these, His own, upon me. Lord, deliver me, yet please not my will!

Friday, August 20

Waiting, all day waiting for that which does not come. All day anticipating some joy, and now tonight seeing it has not arrived and no explanation has been given me. Nothing intentional. It's not a broken promise, but rather a forgotten one. I cannot be hurt; my heart is smiling, truly. For today is my own little motherhood recognized. I am taken for granted; I am forgotten with never a thought of apology. You know what it is, this little innocent oversight. Motherhood is a claim to it. How can he who today forgot me know what a joy it has been? I do love him all the more for it. And I pray that when I, too, am presumptuous, I may cause you this happiness. Let it simply be a proclamation of your motherhood and of my great need of you.

Friday, August 27

Me again, your little one who needs you so. I'm happy for this need, my only treasure. Do take it now and offer it again to the loving Father, Who kindly made me so little and poor.

Saturday, August 28

Each evening I sit here with you, Mother, to hear that which is the first knowledge you gave me, that which will be the last, besides which you'll give no other: Jesus, Jesus, Jesus, the Beginning, the End and the Way. And there is nothing for me but the thrill of this repetition.

Sunday, August 29

Do I smile in my sleep? I should; each heartbeat, breath, every second of life is a proclamation of God's goodness.

Monday, August 30

Just this evening I watched a movie depicting the cruel martyrdom of the early Christians. As I watched those joyous hearts sing themselves to death, I knew that my longing for death is so selfish. And perhaps, for the first time, I preferred suffering a lengthy exile to the too glorious martyrdom I might have fancied for myself at one time. Who is to admire one for rising in the morning, for laughing with the happy, weeping with the sad, pecking notes, visiting, falling asleep? Yet what is my martyrdom but living? This I accept.

Tuesday, August 31

Mother, I just came from the second-floor kitchen, where Betty and I were chatting. It's late. It's wonderful night. If it seems long to another, do let me be of some little assistance in whiling it away. It is never long enough for me. I'm grateful for this deep appreciation of night. Someday there will be only the Son. Till then I'm glad to be hidden from even myself in this darkness. A seed buried deep can better develop sturdy roots. What matter when I break through the soil? Just tell Jesus I am here and His.

Monday, September 6

Surely, in spite of my poverty, I may fill my brothers and sisters who come to me. Please let me be their fullness; how irrelevant that the chalice is emptied. A chalice is made simply to be drained, to serve always, to find fulfillment only in this.

Father Keith sent "the only relic of my First Communion day, the candle stand placed on the altar of St. Philip Church for the occasion." O how I know I am not worthy, not worthy of offering my life that he become ever more Jesus. But because I'll never be worthy of anything, I accept this pain, his love and the humiliation it brings me because I know how unworthy of it I am. Please be tender with him for whom you offer my poverty. Thank you, Mother. In sweet hope I'm glad to live and die for him who ignited an eternal Flame in me.

Saturday, October 2 (Feast of the Holy Guardian Angels)

When both my body and soul were nourished this morning with the Bread of your love, Mother, I was suddenly aware, as I invited my angel guardian to join me in adoring God, of the pain this companion must endure because of me. He who sees God always must at the same instant look upon ME. What apologies and gratitude do I not owe him? Please help me to lessen the difference between these two objects of his solicitude.

With what strange audacity have I made today's requests. My unworthiness kneels before infinite Mercy. Here I long to stay, with a "yes" to each moment's Annunciation.

I'm nearly afraid tonight, afraid of my weakness because it hides such strength. Please plunge me yet deeper into that Furnace that burns away all fear.

Sunday, October 3

Please greet little Thérèse for me. She'd be amused if you would tell her that in the most recent treasure of my crucifixion

I can no longer read even her writings. They once brought such consolation. But this too is gone; not enough is gone. Please help me to leave ALL THINGS to follow my precious Hobo King.

Thursday, October 7

My Queen, O but first and most happily my Mother, I wove a little garland today with which to crown you. Please stoop low that my littleness might reach. There; I knew you'd love it. I've seen my brothers and sisters weaving beads through their fingers and prayers through their lips, and I've truly tried to imitate them. They were beautiful. Will you not take my desires? That's all I ever seem to have for you. But there was something O so special this morning. With my first stir such a stabbing spasm as I've never yet experienced. The least excessive move brought it back. I'm sorry that I couldn't suppress the little whimper it brought, nor the smile. Others probably thought I was giggling. You know, Mother, it used to matter much what others thought. Now I'm glad they know so little, especially those who wryly claim to know our secrets. I need these little things that are so specially yours and mine. So here is the funny little gift and another funny little gift, my love.

Sunday, October 24

It's your poor little hobo once more. Mother, thank you for being here. I'm in such great need; please let me rest here with you. It is late. I returned from two weeks in Gary just this evening. They were beautiful weeks. There were intense sufferings producing great joys, and God's ways remain incomprehensible. So often I find myself shaking my head, muttering "That God!" for want of another phrase, and then, "I think I'll keep Him." Such silliness, boldness, and yet because I'm a child nothing else is expected of me, for I dare and delight to say "Our Father."

I'm quite weak, Mother. And O so restless. It seems I might ask to take some deep breaths without a chest spasm, or that this persistent throbbing in my head be relieved. But Jesus' Cross is founded in my heart and I'll never request that it be removed. Besides, to even be conscious of these while such anguish kisses the depths of my heart is almost impossible. O Woman of the Pietà, please tell Jesus that my arms, too, remain open and waiting for as long as He may choose to keep me in the darkness of that hour in which He saves the world.

It's so hard to think, Mother. I'm so tired. But I needn't think, I know that Love lives. I'm limp with rejoicing; take this whispered alleluia.

Wednesday, October 27

Ruth was here this evening. She has me in my gown and I was all tucked, but the day wasn't quite complete. I need this sweet minute with you. So look, mom, no braces, many wiggles and so very much love for you. The design on my feminine gown forms a cross to cover my whole chest. As you put me to rest in the arms of Our Father tonight, please draw His attention to it. The chest spasms and fatigue hidden under this lace will remind Him of another and — O too wondrous desire — He'll see me and be well pleased.

Friday, October 29

It's so cold, Mother. This morning my muscles were such knots; dressing was a day's labor. And there sat my new heater, still sealed in its box. How can I forget my people here, and how can I possess such luxuries besides? Shoving down the corridor, I passed one of these little ones who was in PAIN from the cold. Yes, there the heater belongs. I'm so glad it's there and in the morning I'll don my goose bumps and sing Lauds.

Monday, November 1
(All Saints' Day)

Only a very little one can be bold and unnoticed. So I've sent my heart to gather all the praise that has ever risen from my brothers and sisters already in their eternal Beatitude to you their Queen, their Mother, and in the scrambled limitations of this note to you I send the love song of all your children.

Tuesday, November 2

Tomorrow I'll go to baffle the fellas at the clinic. Mother, I want so very much from this trip, an end to this ache in my head and eyes; and strength, how I long for just a little more. I'm so tired of forcing my every move. But Jesus knows that already there's a "yes" above these petty wants. Happiness is being so His that I know He can do anything He likes with me!

Monday, November 8

Please help me to make sense to you; I'm too joyously exhausted and confused to understand myself. You know, Jesus knows, how totally I became my little brother Charles' words, "For the sake of the Gospel, I'm willing to go to the ends of the earth and to live till time is no more." What miracles did God not have to work in my poverty to wrench this from me? I know it is here and I stand back and marvel. And I know that it is here irrevocably; there is no retreat from this surrender.

Yes, I shall go wherever my Hobo King leads me, and shall live till the last accomplishment of the words "Thy Kingdom come!" are drained from me. Yet because I know I am ready for this, I know even more certainly that Home is soon, and it's there that I'll begin the apostolate that is designed in exile to be but one seed in a desert.

Mother, you know your little one is a bit frightened. Why is the unknown such a monster to us? My Beloved is the true

Unknown. I'm frightened at the prospect of enduring what I was blessed with six years ago, of the physical and then the mental oblation. [*Virginia is referring to her severe illness during her senior year in high school, which prompted her act of complete abandonment to God.*] But tonight, for each second that I might not remember it, I give the most joyous and total YES that my poverty has ever uttered, and I'm glad that it is you who fling me totally and incessantly into the Living Love that is God.

Wednesday, November 10

This evening I am completely voiceless. It is a sweet situation, for there is such an affinity with the tongueless ones. I lift my eyes to Beauty too great for their endurance, and beg mercy and wait in total confidence.

Monday, November 15

In Jesus' words to us today, He tells us that we're salt and we're light. It's another of those paradoxes our Master of fairy tales has spun. We must take care that we lose not our flavor. Does this not mean reading, time alone with Him, days in the desert? And again He says that our light must shine before all men. We'll be consumed by their hunger! Yet so truly I live, not I. How Jesus longed to be alone with His Father. His every hiding place was discovered, and He embraced those hungry little lambs. His restless Heart knows how my own is torn; I'm so glad He and He alone knows. This is ours, and the multitudes will not take that suffering from me. It is the only thing they will not take and it is the only thing worth keeping, the only giving in me. Blessed be His exquisite, incomprehensible design!

Friday, December 3

The night of December 1st, the anniversary of the martyrdom of our little brother Charles, I was at the Little Sisters' fraternity in Chicago. In the poverty of that tenement building, with roaches creeping everywhere, we spent half the night together in adoration before the Bread of Life you prepared for us with the warmth of your very heart. Thank you for so precious a family! It seems I should be able to write volumes to you this evening, but Love's simplicity has made me pressure even this much from the depths, from the fullness of Jesus that is poured into us. Please forgive my ignorance in even trying to express what you alone know of the mysteries in Divine Humanity. He Who is Life is vibrating every fiber of my heart, and with the cries of anguish this evokes, I fling the whisper of my praise into the peal of your *Magnificat*.

Saturday, December 4

Please, Mother, I beg you to hasten the establishment of Jesus' Kingdom in the desert of my heart. I am desire; when will be fulfillment?

Saturday, December 11

I know Jesus is coming; it's been years since I've endured such pain. Last time I went to the clinic I was intending to ask if I might do without my body brace; it had been so long since I'd had any difficulty with my back. But now the sciatic nerve is singing from my fingertips to my toes. I'm afraid to rest; it but increases my weakness. And yet there is such an irritation in me. I'm so scared it will pounce upon someone almost without my knowledge. Do help me to keep it, all of it, for Jesus. In this darkness His star can better shine. As I fall so often to the floor and must lie there gathering strength to pull myself up, please let the fall of God from His majesty and His rejection among His poor creatures be a little less harsh.

Please, transparent one, hide me. And remind Our Father that I am of the earth and of men, and His Son is my King. He Who is Love will hear you.

Sunday, December 12

I cry out for that river of peace promised at the coming of Jesus, and if that river is but the flow of my tears of abandonment, it is a grateful little heart that weeps.

Saturday, January 22, 1966

Mother, please tell me again you hear me in this exile. I asked you to make of my poor heart your Baby's cradle; why am I surprised that it is so heavy? It bears Him Who bears all. Mother — so long since I last had these dear moments with you, and is there nothing to say? God speaks a Word; do I dare violate It with my own? No Mother, here I am and I am your Child. This is enough; anything less will never be enough.

Sunday, January 23

It's a long time since I could toss a jest down the corridor, could use the phone and forget the miracle that another heard, could stop and chatter a little with my old folks instead of posing a smile or a kiss. Yet somehow I find this voicelessness very dear. Please let me hear more; lend me your compassion so that little ones may rest in the knowledge that another understands and bears with them their gifts. Pray that I become the Word whose Mother you are.

Thursday, January 27

Mother dear, tomorrow will find me a patient at St. Joseph Memorial Hospital. What shall I find? What beauteous horrors will bruise my eyes and my ears as I lie there? Please, you so unmercifully schooled in this, help me to be a "savior with Jesus."

Wednesday, February 2

Here's your little one again. It's SO good to be up and ever so slowly pecking a note to you. Mother, I am very weak. Doc permitted me no time out of bed except that spent on the commode. At first it seemed a terrible existence. Why is my faith so slow to perceive all these miracles around me? Pinned there in total helplessness, there was a world to save with Jesus.

No, my voice is no better; with the rest of my body the vocal cords have grown weak. How long must I wait for a voice? I have no idea, and it truly concerns me far less than this crushing fatigue. But I AM Jesus' little hobo. Please assure Him that whenever He calls, though every fiber of my body threatens rebellion, my heart can but follow Him and rest in nothing less than tearing down every obstacle till I at last find Him and am consumed in what I've found.

Saturday, February 5

While reciting this evening's Vespers, my voice became unusually strong, and aloud I read each word. I came upstairs tingling at this new volume and greeted the girls nearly boastfully. But now I am very weary again, and there is hardly a squeak left in me. Let me not be presumptuous, nor proud nor hasty. Teach my heart, like yours, to seek to give all that it has to give, and ever more. And mostly, let it first ask my Beloved what gift will delight Him most, and then there will be nothing to keep me from attaining it.

Sunday, February 6

Before dawn a soft, sweet scent wakened me, and when at last I took my first peek at the day, I discovered here in my dear nook a large rose floating in a crystal goblet. Its petals were extended in total surrender, as if it were in a chalice awaiting the words of Transubstantiation. I whispered them over it, knowing that He Who alone was listening would alone understand, "This is my blood!"

Monday, February 7

You, who knew the smell of sheep and the price of eggs, who knew also that beneath your poor roof dwelt Almighty God, were Mary of Nazareth. All knew you thus. Do let me be known as the little Kokomite who, though she is often thrown into other segments of God's milieu, still is happy when she finds herself "of Sam" and of all Sam's burdens. O yes, there are burdens here these days. I've never felt them so, perhaps just because of my own weakness at present. But I'm glad for the weight of them; they tie me here where, for this brief time, I belong.

Sunday, February 13

Jesus in His living Gospel speaks to us today of seeds. I've thought often of all those wondrous promises in His desert. But a little thing that flits about so much as I can't be promising. Can I not be for Him a grain of sand, shifting, whispering what others are made to shout from mountaintops? When His Spirit blows me here and there perhaps the Father will discover a sprout of His Son Who called Himself the Vine and be pleased. To think my restless pilgrimage might please Him so! Mother, I love being this little thing that among millions of others is stained with Brother Charles' blood and Jesus' Love.

Saturday, March 19

Mother, I collapse into your care. After five weeks in another hospital, here I am worse than when I entered. If only there were an explanation. Tell me I am pleasing Jesus; that is enough. And yet perhaps it is more pleasing to Him that I cannot know. So I rest tonight in the insecurity that has always been my one security.

Tuesday, March 22

The audio-aid kit came in today's mail. It looks a little like a man's shaving kit, and inside are two receivers, batteries and controls. The slightest whisper is clearly transmitted. It's such an expensive item I grow ashamed looking at it. For more and more I realize I must become what I used to verbalize. The Word is flesh, and what right have I to keep that Truth secret???

Sunday, March 27

With Jesus today I remembered that Father Keith called me his molting canary. How appropriate. So bedraggled, I without a song, yet still in the cage of Jesus' Love. Even if the door is left ajar, I haven't the strength nor will to fly away. It is enough to wait for warmth and a song to return. And if they evade me for ten lifetimes, still it is enough to know I'm Jesus', that He continues to feed and cleanse me because He wants me to stay. But sometime soon I long for that warm, graceful hand to come that I may perch on its finger and sing again. Still, if it but cares for me without this pause for my selfishness, isn't this enough? "Yes."

Tuesday, March 29

Mother of priests, Queen of our hearts, please help us. Father ___ came last night and will be here till Thursday. O that he were gone now! In all my encounters with those intimately sharing the Priesthood of Jesus Christ I've never encountered this. This afternoon and again this evening he tried to molest me. Though I've often smelt alcohol on his breath, I detected none today. In my voicelessness my poor heart pleaded with Maria Goretti, "God does not will it!" But I am so weak these days, and tonight sheerly exhausted from fighting him off. Please don't let him come in tomorrow. Or may not your little hobo have an outing? You tell me what to do, Mother. Now more than ever I feel the intimacy of my vocation with the Sacred Priesthood. What might I do to help Father? Tell me, please! Yet impotent as I am, I can but beg that YOU do it for me. Will running from him show him the way to true Love? I just don't know; just abandon me to Him Who is Love and I accept tomorrow's wondrous designs.

Wednesday, March 30

This morning I did slip away, Mother, and stayed till three this afternoon. But after supper and Vespers, the same nightmare. I am too weak to fight off this priest turned beast to me, and I've no voice to plead with him nor to cry for help.

As He offered the Holy Sacrifice this morning, it took every ounce of faith in me and that for which I pleaded at the moment: to see Father at the altar and to be in Love with him. My soul is sick just remembering the smell of his body, and I cling to Jesus' ring on my finger and beg for Love. I have only desire; please purify that. I almost complain to Jesus that this is too much, that I am so drained already I can't tolerate this final blow. But here is His strength, and in that alone my fitful thoughts find calm and melt into Love.

Thursday, March 31

Father ___ left this morning, and Jean, Lulu, and I spent an hour with Jesus for our priests. Help them, please.

Annie [*Quentin's sister*] writes, "Easter is going to be fun, not for seeing Quentin, it's you." And in my Peanutty fashion I smile, "Nyahh!" Quentin, Easter will mark the first year of our love. A year, a day and a forever. And since then the nearly painful freedom of our love. I love him so I cannot even attempt to spare him pain, for to give him myself is to inflict so much on him. Quentin of the Cross, I fear I have become that cross for him. In the hands of this priest and victim I am the little host to be broken and consumed. It is good to be here.

In perusing a leaflet, I came across "The Gospel According To You" and the line, "You are probably the only Gospel most people will ever read." My first reaction, "God forbid!" had to be slowly tempered. He's not forbidden it; He's ordained it so. That "yes" does entail so many more, doesn't it? This wrenched another "yes" from me today.

Saturday, April 23 [After Holy Week and Easter at St. Meinrad's]

Mother dear, your little hobo is glad for you and for this night whose rhyme is the peck of a typewriter. I am returned? The word seems inadequate now. Exile has grown to such reality in me that there is no return, nowhere to lay my heart. I follow Him who seeks to requite Love, and there is no rest. I can't deny I knew what a Hobo He was when I accepted His invitation. I am groaning under His yoke and I am smiling. It is sweet, though I could not find words nor thoughts if one were to ask me how. Those matter little. He heard the first yes and heard those following and knew that the final one would not be more frail than the first. Is there any but that first? Sometimes it seems not.

For days I've been in awe at this new contemplation of the Pascal Mystery. "SHALOM!" O the simplicity of it all! During Holy Week I fretted from one exercise to another, desperate to find in its intensity some strength. But there was total confusion. And when I'd exhausted all my energies and fell, forcefully abandoned, to where alone is strength, I found One Who walked upon our earth and spoke my name and gave my body something to eat; One so close His breath is upon our foreheads. And when I yet failed to recognize Him He tearfully spoke my name. There must not be a moment that is not a vocation! YES, LORD.

It's very late. I've just read the mail that piled upon my desk these past weeks, and my heart is heavy. Why so easily burdened? And so filled with joy? *Shalom*, yes, Jesus is so alive and alive am I in the greeting, the Incarnation, of the Word of God.

Monday, April 25

Let me sit still. Even among these rocks, my peace in His Will. I'm so tired, I'm restless and my stomach heaves and my muscles plead for rest and my head pounds its protests while my heart, secure in the knowledge that it has been happily cast into Our Father's strong arms forever, finds futile its attempts to rationalize with my members. They care not for my love of the night and solitude and quiet. Let me forget their silliness and myself entirely in that glorious, though at present totally obscure, certainty that Love Is.

Tuesday, April 26

Strange little things we are, aren't we, Mother dear? We give ourselves "totally" to Jesus, yet each time He asks to claim what is His own we are surprised and struggle sometimes at great length before a reluctant but nonetheless sincere yes is pulled from us. Today I lost my ring. It's been loose for a long time, but I've caught it each time it fell from my finger and quickly replaced it. Today, however, it rolled beneath a radiator and into a crevice I know not how deep. Perhaps it leads to the furnace. I didn't realize how accustomed I'd grown to fingering it and remembering to Whom it wed me. Now all I find is the callus my finger manufactured to keep it there, the callus that just wasn't big enough. Yes, I know this makes me no less His. I'm glad for all it has meant and for this, Jesus' gift to me, which He kindly transforms into mine to give. How little we suspect the Poverty that can at last see Him face-to-face!

Thursday, April 28

"O Lord, receive the pressed grape. May it be your Blood." How long, O how long until it becomes His Blood? Please press me in love's violence to your Immaculate Heart that at last I may be poured out in Jesus' Holy Sacrifice.

Sunday, May 1

"I long for Nazareth" and rejoice to realize that in my heart alone are its secrets, all those wondrous things in the Gospels I fail to realize because I strain to read so well.

Monday, May 2

I'm so, so tired, and my feet swollen, red and sore with a burning pain. Yet what ridiculous aggravations I come up with. This morning, when Father came to distribute the Eucharist, I was so, so anxious to tell Jesus all those wonderful things included in the Amen we return when Father says to us, "The Body of Christ!" But again this morning, after I'd whispered the most expressive Amen I can produce, Sister answered for me. It always seems mine isn't sufficient. My one liturgical act of the day is every day taken from me. Every day I think perhaps my own will be enough, and every day it is snatched from me. The poverty is more nagging because so insignificant. Much more importantly, to the fact that I must be always denied this least of participation, please help me to say "Amen!"

Tuesday, May 3

Speaking has been extremely difficult today, but I'm nearly amazed at my own indifference. It's good to be misinterpreted; it will make me more Jesus.

Saturday, May 7

Today I've been happily lost in the memory of my First Communion. Of course we First Communicants were the first to waken that morning at the Villa, but we were instructed to stay in bed till the other girls had left the washroom. O how we wiggled. Then, after we were all dressed — my dress the very plainest of designs made special by a square lace collar and white shoes — out into that wondrous morning we filed. It had been raining all night, but the sun merely made of the dew that morning so many jewels in our path. I was at the end of the line and remember remarking that I must be careful at the turn in the sidewalk. But still I fell, and my heart too was thrown into the mud. I quickly arose to bear the shame of my fall with me and tugged at my dress till there was no longer an inch to search for mud. Then, with loving presumption, I remembered that I had a very good angel with me and wasn't surprised that she'd cared for me so. Only years later did I remember and, breathless with gratitude, pause long to say thank you. But right then there was something far more important: I was going to the altar of God.

Daddy was in the choir loft that day with the tape recorders, and he said it took him five minutes to find me there among the others, so well did I walk. The Holy Sacrifice seemed so long, the sermon, the prayers we had to recite aloud. One thing was to be desired and at last we approached the Banquet. Thrilled as I was, my first remark to Jesus was, "You choose strange bread in which to come to me." This morning, when I received the same Bread, I tried to imagine what might have been a more preferable greeting, and I found myself repeating the first. I'll always be ignorant before this Manna, the very meaning of which term is "What is it?" For my First Communion, the first in that which is eternal, I want to say thank you. Please do so for me, Mother. I remain your little one.

Today's Gospel has thrilled my poor heart. "If you live your life in me, and my words live in your hearts, you can ask for whatever you like and it will come true for you." Sometimes I want so to ask, yet I don't. Perhaps I know I am not living enough in Jesus, that His words aren't alive enough in my heart. I long for that Life when what I ask and what He wishes are the same because my request is but the necessary expression of His Life in me. Please hasten to accomplish this in me. I accept now the continual death this entails. Please become always more and more my Mother because I am more and more alive with the love you have for Jesus.

Tuesday, May 10

Twenty-four years ago today, He Who "knit me in my mother's womb" brought me into the world. Many call this world cruel, but He looked upon it and smiled with satisfaction because He found it good, so good He sent His beloved Son. To this very same world He has sent me, and for the same reason, for there is no distinction between His Eternal Son's vocation and His little hobo's. "I've come that they may have life . . . abundantly."

Thursday, May 12

A little sleepyhead comes to give you her goodnight "peck." I am tired, but I think it's an effect of the pain pills. I've taken twice as many today than usual. Please don't let them diminish the totality of my gift. Surely our ease is as dear to God as our crucifixion.

Saturday, May 14

My precious SME [*Sister Mary Eugenia*], I got to be with her a few timeless moments today! Upon seeing me, she remarked, "Virginia, I've seen you look better but not happier." I AM happy, Mother; you know that, a happiness nourished on anguish. But to know that she could see it, that she could be happy with me, that it is too much for my littleness and must spill upon those I love, thank God. It's not so much a happiness she recognized as a joy too deep to be diminished, born and growing in a depth where "my hour has come."

Sunday, May 15

Little ones are thirsty; their cries are rending my heart. Yes, Mother dear, I am still their little cup. Let them drain me, even though that means turning me upside down. Let me be theirs in the shadow of that folly with which Jesus is mine.

Tuesday, May 17

John Kiefer requested for his graduation gift a letter. This morning, as I tried to fulfill that request, I realized I could throw no more of myself into that letter than the one I'd just written to a little third grader. Each correspondent is worthy of a total gift; let me never be lukewarm. If the "pen is mightier than the sword," what then of the typewriter? Yet I cannot tremble before this machine; that would accomplish nothing. I throw myself upon Jesus' Love and know no task — nothing — is beyond His strength that is my own.

Wednesday, May 18

Mother of my insecurity, take my unshed tears; take me please. This restlessness has robbed me of myself; when will you finally give me to my Beloved? Blessed be the Love whose roots are deep and hidden in this slow, anonymous repeating host of days.

Thursday, May 19

How alone we must become to realize our union with Jesus. My "desert" today was a barren experience. Heaven is Jesus; there is no hell but the self we so often serve. There is only one beatitude, the happiness of my Beloved eternally united to His Father. Just a few minutes ago, the aide working this night shift asked me if I was happy. With tears in my heart I almost sang an obvious yes, because Jesus is happy. That is all I have left to make me smile, yet to smile because of anything else would be to don a mask.

Truly there is nothing God does not wish to give us; O to learn the gracious art of receiving. Let the reception and the return of all gifts be but one movement of our love.

Sunday, May 29

Mother darling, I am so tired. It seems eating, sleeping, resting, nothing relieves this fatigue. Perhaps at last I'm beginning to realize this just might be my lot till I get Home. It is a difficult thing to face myself with. Rest, everyone says, but I'm scared to rest. I know it will bring nothing but greater weakness. And surely Jesus wants me to use all these gifts to the full. When they are entirely exhausted, then they will have been spent in Our Father's business, and I want nothing more. From the depths I cry, "How long?" Please transform even this into a plea that God's Kingdom come. If I close this letter with a nostalgic, "I wanna go Home," I'll not forget the P.S.: my prayer of abandonment.

Monday, July 4

The mounting number of my correspondents nearly frightens me. Surely there are 300; I've not counted them recently. The responsibility is weighty, I so weak, so tired, and Jesus so strong, so alive. Please thank Him for each of them. I know there is not one I don't need, not one who doesn't somehow stoop to need me. Love doesn't inquire how, but remains restless until crucifixion.

Tuesday, July 5

It rained a little this evening; now there's a slight breeze playing about my corner. Think I'll hurry to prepare for the night and let it dart through my toes.

Wednesday, July 6

Our Sister Alexis lies with us tonight so very near Home. She's waited long, slowly being stripped of all things that at long last she might see God. See that her entrance to Him is glorious, and perhaps tell her to ask of Him Who awaited her so long, a favor for one she always knew here as "the child."

Friday, July 8

God so great; my heart so narrow. Please, though He'll have to break it, tell Him to make it the abode of His Love.

Sunday, July 24

Me again, and again I love you. What is to be said of the past two weeks? My heartstrings have been busy, and upon them ballads from the depths of me to my God.

It was good to have to leave Velma's today. There is too much peace, comfort, security there. You know, Mother, I could so easily let go of everything there. I find myself not fighting but floating. And the minute I cease to use force, weakness pounces upon me. There seems to be no middle road. I must drive myself to every move, eat twice as much as I want, go, go, go, peck letter after letter, nothing but Brother Charles' "Dread is the sign of duty," to goad me on, or I quit. Would it really be wrong to quit? I've asked myself that question often, and each time Jesus shows me some little servant girl digging a hole in the ground to bury her talent. That answer is clear enough.

Monday, July 25

Good night; it truly is. Everything is still. Please obtain for your little ones eternal rest someday and the love to go on and on and on until that someday.

Tuesday, July 26 (Feast of St. Anne)

Today we remember especially YOUR mother. Please tell me about her. Tell me what you did together, the things you talked about. Most of all, tell me how you loved her, how you expressed that love. You know I love you; tell me how to truly love a mother. How else can I know? And how else can I become more and more Jesus?

Saturday, July 30

Mother darling, I'm so restless tonight. Some nagging pain in my arms and legs and head has been robbing me of late. I've just returned from a good talk with our new aide who is with us during the lonely hours; it was good and I'm glad tonight isn't for sleep. Soon the Lord's Day will begin. Please help me to get dressed in time and to be as attentive as I should to His speech and His silence. Surely it will be no less His day than this has been His night. Abandon me now to Infinite Kindness.

Sunday, July 31

Please help me to say a total yes to the call of Jesus, even though it be not understood by others or perhaps by myself.

Monday, August 1

Speaking has become so burdensome to me, yet how very often I break silence for something trivial, how very seldom is there something worthy of breaking silence. Please quiet my heart as Jesus has quieted my voice.

Thursday, August 4

"Do with me what You will." But who am I to demand [*to know*] just what He plans to do? Please help me, someday, to say and truly say my prayer of abandonment, even though it be, "My God, my God, why have You forsaken me!"

Friday, August 5

So many, many things I thought were cumbersome I see now were but there to keep me from falling. I begged that I be rid of those nuisances; my prayer has been answered, and here I stand in some black abyss, the noise of my fretting all there is now to be called distraction. Where am I; is this really Love? And I find myself wondering if I've ever truly known Love. Mother, please help me. No, I'm not afraid. I know that of the words our beloved Lord and Brother taught us to say, the first are "Our Father."

Saturday, August 6

Today's feast is so precious to me. Transfiguration. God leads me to climb His holy mountain, alone, and when I've reached its peaks, too exhausted to encumber myself with any-thing, I drop my empty hands and lift my eyes, and though I am blinded, my soul knows He Is Who Is and is refreshed, is transfigured itself. How can His glory be hidden? Yet I don't reveal it to others. Please make me His living Gospel.

Sunday, August 7

I've lived and loved another day. Now I'll hop into my nightie and wait to greet our eleven o'clock aide, then abandon everything to Omnipotence and sleep. Goodnight, my darling Mother; I love you.

Wednesday, August 10

I've been sitting here dozing again. Please don't let me make this a habit; for several nights now I've fallen asleep on my typewriter. Let me prepare for bed when I should and please don't let me slip into laziness. It's too easy, and I WANT to follow Jesus. You know how much I want to, Mother. Nothing, not even this fatigue, must slow me. Please help; I know I am so dependent upon you and this is my glory. This is your Maternity made painfully, wondrously tangible to me. Thank God for me, please.

Wednesday, August 24

It's time to be tired, and I am. But Mother, it was a good day. Love always makes it so. I believe in love; please fill my disbelief.

Saturday, September 3

My "whisper phone" must be returned, I learned by a certified letter today. Strange that I let go of it with such hesitancy. I've not used it much, yet there were times when it was so convenient. Now more than ever is my opportunity to become what I wish to say, to let others know the Word is flesh. *Fiat*.

nine

❦

OCTOBER 4, 1966, to NOVEMBER 18, 1966

Virginia receives a letter from the priest who molested her, asking forgiveness. On October 15th, she learns to her great relief that individuals with her type of cerebral palsy rarely live to the age of twenty-five. As Virginia gets weaker, the aides at Good Sam receive orders to help her less. Typical of the constant battle between fatigue and determined Love is her entry of October 25th. She writes, "I'm so tired, Mother, your little unprofitable one, unless profit be found in regions where my weariness won't let me search. That doesn't matter; tonight I'm so yours, and use the little strength left in me to smile."

+

LOVE

Saturday, October 8, 1966

A note from Father ___ today. Somehow it's like the return of a nightmare that has never really stopped frightening me. He asks me to write to him; I shall. Forgive him? I've never found this necessary. There is but pity and horror and an impelling desire to be ever more a sacrifice for priestly priests.

Sunday, October 9

It's night and quiet, and there is but the song of raindrops to sing my own voiceless song of unshed tears.

Tuesday, October 11

Today, Holy Mother Church celebrates your Divine Maternity. I love this feast, though in my heart's liturgy it is rather perpetual. There is nothing I delight in calling you more than "Mother." My beloved Lord and Brother Jesus Christ must have pressed this, His own delight, so indelibly upon my poor heart. I'm glad.

Saturday, October 15

Today we celebrate the feast of our precious sister, St. Teresa [of Ávila]. Somehow I knew this morning she had much in store for her little sister who loves her so. O Mother, all this time I've felt so guilty about my laziness, listlessness, irritability. I've pushed and pushed and become irritated at my constant failures to meet the goals I set for myself; goals I once attained so easily. And at last I've heard what I've suspected all along. During my sojourn in the hospital it was disclosed that people with my particular case of CP seldom live over twenty-five years. Mother, do you know what this means? All this time I've been told CP is not progressive, and I felt as one who must have buried her talent somewhere, so I dug and dug trying to regain it, weeping because it was nowhere to be found. Every time I gain a pound or someone tells me how good I'm looking I condemn myself because my activity doesn't correspond. Mother, this knowledge is liberation from this torment. Each day I'll give my all, but when I examine it, when others criticize my dwindling offering, I'll rest in the peace of knowing it is my all and it is no longer mine but Jesus'. Please thank Teresa for this liberation sent on her feast day, and ask her to let me soar with her to the sweet, agonizing furnace of Love.

Friday, October 28

Please let love transform everything into adoration.

Wednesday, November 2

It's late again, I know, Mother. Once more I was too exhausted to prepare for bed, so fell asleep here in my wheelchair, my head on the keyboard of the typewriter. It happens too often, Mother. O I wish the girls could help me in the evening. The days are long and big, each of them. But I know Sister has told the aides to let me care for myself, so don't let me ask of them what they've been told not to do. Yet, sometimes I must. Forgive me and reward their loving hearts that jeopardize a job for the sake of kindness.

Thursday, November 3

Your little sleepyhead has but a nod for you tonight, and she's glad Mothers are glad for little things.

Friday, November 4

It's your little clown. All day I've been typing with one numb finger, just one. The other day it was my bottom lip that felt so large and let everything dribble. What a silly little thing you call your child. O but I know you do love me, and I'm glad, and long to respond totally to that love.

[*Shortly after this entry, Virginia was admitted to St. Joseph Hospital in Elwood because of her weakening condition. While at the hospital, she was invited by Ruth and Ted Kiefer to stay with their family. The last entry of Virginia's "Letters to Mother" was dictated to Ruth Kiefer, so the original is in Ruth's handwriting.*]

November 18

Once upon Eternity
Mother darling,

It is not evening. Or perhaps it is more dark than it has ever been when I pecked a love note to you. You see that I am not writing this myself. It is not my own now to exercise that child's privilege. So many things I presumed to use so freely, sometimes so forgetfully, are gone. Please don't find in me a note of surprise or objection. Rather, there is some silent *Magnificat* where your own song of praise was sung long before Elizabeth heard it.

There is so much screaming for expression, yet I've just had a friend mimeograph a letter to my dear ones. I shall not be writing to them. But perhaps they will see an empty corner or one wilted red rose and remember, and know with a new certainty the Word is flesh.

And you, Mother? You know as no one else of my love. You understand. I'm so grateful for your care, and feel it's quite unnecessary to ask my Mother to continue making me what I have always asked to be, only Jesus.

Now I give [*you*] the last of these "scraps of useless paper."
I wonder if somewhere there is someone who will write to you
and know how much you are MOTHER.

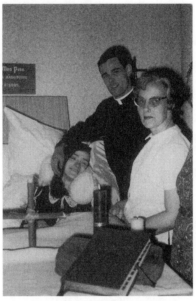

Virginia, Father Keith, and Ruth
Kiefer, December 24, 1966

Epilogue

❦

February 26, 1967

My dear Frater Quentin,

It is my understanding that you have requested notes and letters from any of the many, many friends and acquaintances of Little Virginia Cyr of Jesus. With your kind indulgence, I will attempt to put some of my thoughts and experiences on paper.

I title my relationship with Little Virginia "The Great Privilege."

For many weeks before Virginia's death, my wife Shirley and I had heard from several of our friends about a very saintly young girl afflicted with cerebral palsy. To hear these people talk, I was led to believe that she had the power to reach inside you, pull from you your soul, examine it and mold it to make it more pleasing to God before putting it back. We had heard how priests came to her bedside to celebrate the Holy Sacrifice of the Mass literally at her feet. We heard of the wisdom that flowed from her lips, of the love that radiated from her entire being. I was particularly impressed with the awe and reverence that seemed to be associated with her very name: "Little Virginia of Jesus."

Since Christmas, I was told, Virginia was steadily going downhill. It was apparent that her suffering was a great concern to everyone — but her. Almost daily, most conversations eventually led to Virginia; and with each passing day I felt I knew her, although I had never met her. My actions were inevitable! Shirley didn't want to meet her. Knowing that she was, physically, a pitiful sight to see, she wanted to keep the image of Virginia that she had imagined. Shirley said once that when she gazed at the huge crucifix in church, she imagined Virginia's face on the figure of Christ. How astoundingly accurate this was, and how fitting. Virginia made her suffering as Christlike as any human could.

I am a florist. We own a small flower and gift shop, and two of Virginia's close friends had each sent a large candle to her, decorated with Christmas trimmings. I was deeply flattered to hear that the candles I had designed were used on the altar — at the foot of her bed — for her private Midnight Mass. Three priests concelebrated Mass while she and her newly adopted family, the Ted Kiefers, participated. When I learned of this, I was deeply moved. This was perhaps one of the deciding events in making up my mind to meet her. I had sent word to find out if she would see me, and, of course, the answer was yes. So on Thursday morning, January 26th, I decorated a very large white candle with white cupids and pink roses. I lit the candle that morning in my store and offered the little flame reaching to heaven for Virginia's own intentions.

Our meeting was strange and beautiful and very significant. I was afraid of showing any sympathy or pity, so I had made up my mind to literally jabber, to avoid any lull in conversation. I nearly made an ass of myself because of the persistent jabbering, but not to Virginia. As I walked into her room, our eyes met, and she radiated with love. I was disappointed for a moment at her tormented disfigurement, but it was a fleeting moment. Her eyes did truly love me. Their depth pierced my soul and I *think* I could feel her caressing little hands gently molding my soul. I don't remember what I said during that hour; I just babbled. It probably wasn't necessary; I prefer to believe that our souls carried on a conversation, and when I left . . . I was full! Full of a closeness to God that I had never known before that day.

She told Ruth Kiefer after I left that the burning candle was her, and when it burned out, she would also burn out. I didn't go back for a few days, but most of my thoughts were in her room.

The following Tuesday, I heard that she was in grave condition and everyone knew her time was near. Wednesday, I tried to prevent the inevitable by taking her a new candle. I lit the new one before extinguishing the nearly burned-out candle that had melted in such a peculiar way. She said the first candle had character and personality, and it amused her to watch the unusual positions it took while it burned day and night. Virginia knew why I had brought the new candle, and her eyes thanked me. The women attending her said she brightened up for the first time in days. I hope that's true; it comforts me.

Virginia at the Kiefers'

Our beloved Father Keith Hosey was there on that Wednesday, and had planned a Mass at her feet. What a privilege to be asked to participate! Here I was with the two people on earth who meant "Christ" to me. What a thrill! Father Hosey said the Mass of the following day, The Blessing of Candles, and the new candle was used in the ancient Liturgy. I began realizing that I was brought to Virginia for a purpose. I watched Virginia during Mass. I watched her body twist and jerk and the veins nearly burst on her thin little face as she suffered through the reenactment of the crucifixion. Have you ever witnessed a martyrdom? All who participated in Mass with Virginia did!

Later that day, that evening and the next morning, people — many people — stopped in to visit and to pray. Virginia had asked that we pray for the end, and everyone was [*praying*].

On Thursday morning Shirley sent two candles, newly blessed at Mass, but Virginia was not aware of much of anything that was going on. She did say that morning, while the women were bathing and changing her, "Tomorrow I will be a bride." I was deeply impressed by these words. Only a sainted person could experience such a beautiful yet agonizing death. Her pain was unbelievably brutal. Why, God? Why don't you take her? I suppose she was still giving the last few ounces of strength left in her body to someone she loved.

Many tears were shed in her room that day and that night by oh so many people who loved this wretched disfigured symbol of love. That night was indeed a long and painful vigil for Virginia and the women who never left her side during her last few days of life.

Shortly before dawn on Friday, February 3, 1967, Little Virginia Cyr of Jesus made her wedding vows for all eternity. Tears were shed by many of her friends, including myself, but only because we would miss her. There was also a great feeling of joy that spread rapidly to all who knew and loved her. Virginia was dead, alleluia!

Virginia was to lie in state in her very own room in the Kiefers' home. There were very few floral tributes, but it was again my great privilege to make the few significant ones that were there. The most magnificent of all was her " 'Charlie' Heart," slightly altered to fit the occasion. A three-foot heart of red carnations *pierced* by a five-foot cross. A crown of thorns encircled the top of the cross, while a representation of the Holy Spirit perched atop the heart for all to behold. The card read: "You made it, Charlie!"

Virginia's crude cross, constructed of two branches tied with twine, a gift to her from you, her beloved Frater Quentin, was placed in her casket. We entwined three red roses around this cross — three for the Trinity, red for love.

Finally, Shirley's and my gift and tribute to this momentous occasion was a crude and rugged cross of bark, garlanded with greens for life. A braided rope hung like the shroud of Christ with each knot to signify a trying step of Virginia's life on earth, all the symbols of life centered by death — Virginia's bridal bouquet. Such a great privilege for me to be such an important part of the final tribute to her.

Virginia's funeral was not her funeral. It could very well have been her wedding. As you know, Frater, eight priests concelebrated Mass vested in white. At the Offertory, a crown of velvet, red roses and hyacinth blossoms was placed on her coffin to signify the crown she received at the Throne of the Almighty. Again, it was my great privilege to construct the crown. Before Virginia was processed to the hearse that would carry her far from us to her grave, we sang, "Alleluia, the strife is over," to the glory of Him who had taken her.

For most in attendance, it was over. A great experience, a beautiful friendship, a loved one gone, the end of suffering or maybe just a witness to a first. But for me it was the beginning of fulfillment. I went to work filled with grief, for I knew that this was the day and the only day that I must meet my confessor face-to-face, something I had avoided since I first met and loved Father Keith Hosey. The decision was the most difficult thing I have ever experienced. Virginia knew it, and this was her gift to me. A new life. At 5:30 the afternoon of Virginia's funeral, I sat face-to-face with my Christ-on-earth, Father Keith. I was afraid as I looked into his eyes filled with love. "Father, this is my first Confession!"

May the blessings of all the saints and Virginia of Jesus be with you, who also loved her.

JIM MCDANIEL

For More Information

~~❧~~

*F*or more information about Virginia Cyr, consult the Web site dedicated to her memory at *http://www.ohiodominican.edu/~colganq*. To report favors granted through the intercession of Virginia, e-mail Dr. Quentin Colgan at the address listed on Virginia's Web site.

Our Sunday Visitor ...
Your Source for Discovering
the Riches of the Catholic Faith

Our Sunday Visitor has an extensive line of materials for young children, teens, and adults. Our books, Bibles, pamphlets, CD-ROMs, audios, and videos are available in bookstores worldwide.

To receive a FREE full-line catalog or for more information, call **Our Sunday Visitor** at **1-800-348-2440, ext. 3**. Or write **Our Sunday Visitor** / 200 Noll Plaza / Huntington, IN 46750.

Please send me ___ A catalog
Please send me materials on:
___ Apologetics and catechetics
___ Prayer books
___ The family
___ Reference works
___ Heritage and the saints
___ The parish

Name _____
Address _____ Apt._____
City _____ State _____ Zip_____
Telephone (   ) _____

                                                             A43BBBBP

Please send a friend ___ A catalog
Please send a friend materials on:
___ Apologetics and catechetics
___ Prayer books
___ The family
___ Reference works
___ Heritage and the saints
___ The parish

Name _____
Address _____ Apt._____
City _____ State _____ Zip_____
Telephone (   ) _____

                                                             A43BBBBP

OurSundayVisitor

200 Noll Plaza, Huntington, IN 46750
Toll free: **1-800-348-2440**
Website: www.osv.com